BE YOUR OWN CHANAKYA

(26 LEADERSHIP LESSONS)

RENU SAINI

PRABHAT PRAKASHAN

Published by
PRABHAT PRAKASHAN PVT. LTD.
4/19 Asaf Ali Road,
New Delhi-110002 (INDIA)
e-mail: prabhatbooks@gmail.com

ISBN 978-93-5521-927-5
BE YOUR OWN CHANAKYA
(26 Leadership Lessons)
by *Renu Saini*

Edition
First, 2023

Price
₹ 350 (Rupees Three Hundred Fifty Only)

Printed at
Japan Art, Delhi

Dedicated to the great strategist and scholar Chanakya who blessed the entire mankind by gifting a wonderful work like 'Arthashastra' to this world.

Author's Note

Newton had once said that nature was a book written in the language of mathematics. Mathematics is a subject that is primarily based on equations, formulae and symbols. A person who masters these equations, formulae and symbols with the help of his knowledge and intelligence finds mathematics quite easy and interesting. On the contrary, mathematics becomes a very difficult and burdensome subject for the one who is unable to properly understand those equations and symbols. Life is also something like that. Life is full of challenges. Some people see these challenges as opportunities, while others treat them as problems. The same word 'Challenge' gives rise to different meanings to different people depending on their understanding.

One who sees a challenge as an opportunity gets motivated towards his karma, while the person treating the same as a problem keeps looking towards his fate. This is where a tussle starts between karma and fate. Those who convert every obstacle into a golden reward, looking at their challenges as opportunities, never agree to accept the doctrine of fate. On the other hand, people treating challenges as problems are not ready to renounce fate and take up karma. And this is how karma and fate are always kept intertwined. Howsoever, the losers may keep on weaving the fabric of fate, the same materialises only when it is given some shape. And a shape can always be sculpted only with the help of karma. Knitting something with wool and needles can never be accomplished until the same is given a desirable shape.

Chanakya, through his monumental work 'Arthashastra' and his various policies, has made an attempt to convey the same concept to everybody that agility, ingenuity, education and good behaviour are essential for any kind of life, be it that of a warrior or a householder, that of a student or a ruler or that of a common man or a soldier. An educated and intelligent person makes even an impossible thing possible and transforms an unfavourable situation into favourable one. It is generally said that time changes everything but, in reference to intelligent, learned, humble and smashes enlightened people, Chanakya believes such a person changes the time by transforming himself, demolishes old records and makes new ones.

A learned and intelligent person knows how to achieve his goals by giving them positive, rapid, concrete, long-term and distinct forms. Every person just wishes to achieve the goals he has set for himself in his life. In that context, this book will be beneficial for all of you. Where, what and how to use the thoughts propounded by Chanakya in any specific context are all that this book intends to explain to its readers. The purpose of writing this book shall be accomplished even if a single reader is able to make this a medium for uplifting his life and the goals therein to a desired level.

❑

Acknowledgements

To Chanakya: But for the existence of Chanakya, this book would not have become a reality. His personality has taught the entire universe today the finer concepts of politics and economics.

To my parents: Millions of thanks to you! You provided me all the opportunities to learn and study. It's you who kindled a love for books in me. It was your love and support only that helped me develop fascination for books. I could interact with them and learn to feel their magic.

To my elder sister Rakhi Saini: My elder sister has always blessed me with her mother-like love, protection and guidance. She is my greatest admirer and critic at the same time. Her words awaken my self-consciousness and constantly inspire me to do something new and good.

To my daughter Aishni: Her growth is constantly inducing enlightenment in me also. Many of the ideas expressed by me in my writing are actually results of her innocence, impartiality, liveliness and enthusiasm.

To Colonel Late R. K. Dahia: Colonel late R. K. Dahia has played a decisive role not only in imparting power to my personality but also in making my writing more effective and forceful.

To the Late Shakuntla Devi: My aunt, Late Shakuntla Devi, played a huge role in strengthening my personality. While she was alive, her ways and behaviour were beyond my understanding, but today, thinking about them, they seem important to me. Her life, filled with sacrifices, will always be an inspiration for me. Her memories inspire me to this day, to keep moving forward.

❑

Contents

Foundation of Success: Practice

Acharya's Pearls of Wisdom

- *It takes drop by drop to fill a pitcher and drop by drop to even fill a river. Saving penny by penny makes a person rich. Similarly, a person may attain any knowledge if he is determined to practice constantly.*
- *Lethargy and lack of practice impairs the wisdom of even a learned person and ruins his knowledge.*
- *Even a holy scripture becomes poison for a scholar who does not keep practising regularly.*

Practice is Essential

Everybody wants to be successful in life. History is replete with examples of the successful greats. But, were all those people really successful right from their birth? Nobody can be successful right from his birth. Every birth is a result of natural process.

Environment, practice, conditions and adverse circumstances are what make a person proficient in a field and work. World famous scientist Thomas Alva Edison was the author of numerous inventions. Electric bulb was his most significant invention that removed darkness from all the houses and filled them with light. There were many other inventions also to his credit. He did face many failures in his endeavours, but he never took these failures as his defeat, rather he learnt from those experiments and acknowledged that his constant practice had contributed to his maturity and made him proficient in his life. It's practice and practice only that helps one to flourish and attain proficiency. One who has the ability to practise does not need anything else to grow. He is sure to somehow attain everything he desires by means of his practice.

Chanakya maintains that even a learned scholar, who has not gone through adequate practice does not possess the ability to recite the sacred scriptures properly and thus becomes an object of ridicule. Similarly, even a simple job becomes very difficult in the absence of constant practice whereas practice makes even the most difficult job simple, easy and exciting. Chanakya was very clever, hard working and pragmatic ever since his very childhood. At every stage of his growth, he assimilated vital experiences that were essential to mould the personality of any individual. Practice is just one of those experiences.

Best Age for Practice

Childhood is the best time to learn and practise anything. A child is quite pliant and extremely receptive in his tender age. He tries to understand every activity on the grounds of reality and then invests his labour with all sincerity to excel in the same. Right from Arjuna of Dwapara Yuga to Sachin Tendulkar of Kaliyuga - they are all typical examples of the same. Many a time, a person remains deprived of all-importance practice in his childhood due to environmental and circumstantial compulsions. However, in such a case, he may still learn the jobs even in his adolescence, youth or adulthood.

Childhood is the best time to learn and practice anything. A child is quite pliant and extremely receptive in his tender age. He tries to understand every activity on the grounds of reality and then invests his labour with all sincerity to excel in the same. Right from Arjuna of Dwapara Yuga to Sachin Tendulkar of Kaliyuga - they are all typical examples of the same.

What is Practice?

A practice is the action of performing an activity repeatedly and constantly over time. Initially, any work may seem torturous and painful, but in fact, this torture and pain is the beginning of success and achievement in disguise. The discomfort, pain, unease and gloom that a person experiences during initial phase of learning something are actually means of moulding the body and mind of that person into a meticulous shape. This is just like physical exercise where also the initial few days of activity results in continuous pain and discomfort prompting the person to even consider discontinuing the same. However, sustained exercise for some more days makes the body habituated to the same and, after some time, the person is able to attain excellence to the extent that people are filled with awe seeing him perform difficult exercises or tasks.

When a task is performed repeatedly for multiple times, it gets automated and, because of constant practice, the person enjoys doing the same. Let's understand this with an example. A piano has 88 keys and a scale has just 8 notes. Still, an expert pianist is able to play the same 88 keys to create different and beautiful melodies every time. How does he do that? He is able to do that as he has mastered the ways to mould those keys and notes in any desired fashion, thanks to his constant practice. Not only that, practice may even enable a person to aim at a target with his eyes closed. Even a blind person may become world famous on account of his excellence achieved by practice.

Jose Feliciano was born in Puerto Rico. Unfortunately, he was born blind. People used to taunt him and make fund of him because of his blindness. He was sometimes even told to go with a begging bowl. However, Jose Feliciano just ignored people's ridicule and focused on practice as an essential part of his life.

Jose Feliciano was born in Puerto Rico. Unfortunately, he was born blind. People used to taunt him and make fun of him because of his blindness. He was sometimes even told to go with a begging bowl. However, Jose Feliciano just ignored people's ridicule and focussed on practice as an essential part of his life. He found an old guitar somewhere. He kept on practising on that guitar day in and day out. His practice used to be so intense sometimes that his fingers would even start bleeding. Today, the entire world knows Jose Feliciano as a renowned guitarist.

It's on account of their continuous practice only that Janhavi of Samalkha in Haryana, Upasana of Abohar in Punjab and Google girl Zia are startling the entire world with their amazing talents.

How much to practise, ideally?

Chanakya asserts that lethargy and lack of practice impair the wisdom of even a learned man and ruin his knowledge. Hence, one should keep practising. If Chanakya has really laid so much emphasis on practice, what should be the duration of practice? Should a person keep practising for life? If a person keeps practising for life, when and how would he be able to become proficient in what he does? These are the questions that are sure to come in the minds of people after reading all this.

If a person practises any specific activity for 3 hours every day, he would have done a total practice of 1095 hours in 365 days i.e. one year. Thus, he would take around nine to ten years to attain a total practice of 10,000 hours. A person may increase or decrease this period according to his needs.

Psychologists and specialists are of the opinion that a person needs to ensure quality practice for around 10,000 hours to reach the highest level of proficiency. This rule of 10,000 hours is applicable to everybody be it a sprinter or an actor or a painter or a writer or a musician or even a scientist. If a person practises any specific activity for 3 hours every day, he would have done a total practice of 1095 hours in 365 days i.e. one year. Thus, he would take around nine to ten years to attain a total practice of 10,000 hours. A person may increase or decrease this period according to his needs.

If a person diligently completes practice for 10,000 hours, there is nothing that would prevent him from attaining his desired goal.

Hence, Chanakya laid a lot of emphasis on practice. It was he who had installed the brave, clever and serene Chandragupta Maurya on the throne of Pataliputra after removing the immoral, tyrannical and cruel ruler Dhanananda. In order to make Chandragupta Maurya worthy for the throne, Chanakya made him practise all the tasks including those involving politics and administration until he attained proficiency in all of them. History knows that Chandragupta Maurya laid the foundation for a new and one of the largest empires on Indian subcontinent. This would not have been possible without practice.

Result is Dependent on the Speed of Practice

Do you know what's the most common response of the candidates successful in 10th and 12th standard examinations and top-level competitive tests when asked about the primary reason for their success? It is 'Practice'! Practice makes even a difficult subject look simple and easy. On the contrary, even a very simple subject becomes incomprehensible if the same is not practised regularly. The speed of practice determines the outcome. The result may be amazing if the speed of practice is fast. At the same time, a slow rate of practice will lead to a slower outcome only.

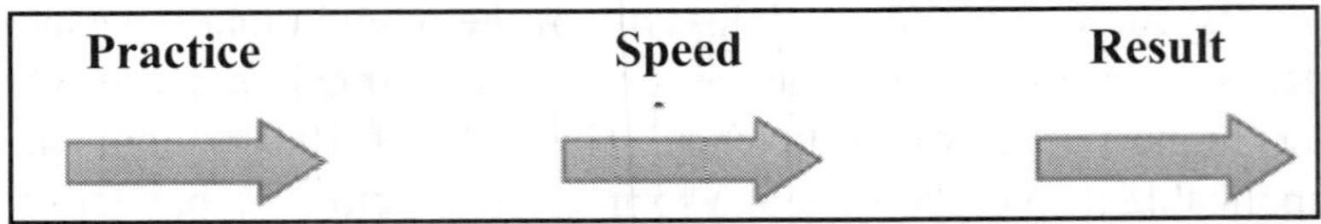

Lessons from Chanakya

Practice is essential for everybody, be it a learned person or an illiterate, a child or an old man, a woman or a man. The more one practises, the more success he achieves. Practice makes one's life perfect and helps him attain unimaginable prosperity and eminence. Chanakya also advises to practise constantly. If a scholar keeps himself away from practice, he finds even the holy scriptures venomous. On the other hand, even a person with average talent may become knowledgeable with practice.

❑

Education: A Rudder of Life

Acharya's Pearls of Wisdom

Knowledge is like the divine cow Kamadhenu. Just as a person having Kamadhenu can never die of hunger, a person, after acquiring knowledge, becomes capable of facing any crisis in life. It is knowledge only that protects a person in a foreign land at every step like a mother. It is knowledge only that is a secret wealth that can't be stolen. On the other hand, the more it is used, the more it grows.

Age No Bar for Acquiring Knowledge

Knowledge is a kind of asset that plays a decisive role in acquiring all other wealth. A learned person is comparatively more matured, prudent and cultured. Knowledge refines mind, untangles the same and motivates it to progress in a new direction. Education and learning have been considered to be of great value ever since ancient times. Satya Yuga, Treta Yuga, Dwapara Yuga, and Kali Yuga - acquiring knowledge has always been given special emphasis in every Yuga. Knowledge does not only cover understanding of books, rather it includes proficiency and skills in practical affairs also. Study of arms and weapons and forms of art makes a person proficient in those respective fields. A person keeps learning during his entire life time. It's learning that ultimately makes him erudite. One who does not learn or stops learning actually comes to the end of his life. His age loses its significance in such a situation. Whether he is 15 years old or 65 years old, a person who stops learning or refuses to learn turns senile. There is no age bar for acquiring knowledge. A person may keep learning and utilise his knowledge as long as he is alive.

Chanakya's father Chanaka was also a teacher. He understood the importance of education and hence motivated his son towards the same. After completing his education at Taxila, Chanakya got appointed as a teacher there itself. He used to explain the principles of economics and philosophy with very pragmatic approach. Having been motivated towards education at a very early age, he understood the importance of the same quite well.

At the age of 96 years, Karthiyani from Kerala has secured the top position in the examination conducted by the Kerala Government under its Literacy Mission Programme. She scored 98 out of 100 marks. Karthiyani's spirit once again demonstrates that age is no bar for learning. For a determined and focused mind, even the most difficult science becomes simple and easy.

It's Best to Start Learning From Childhood

A person would keep getting quite rational if he starts learning from his childhood. Chanakya himself had started reading Vedas at his early age. He even attained proficiency in Vedas at a very tender age. Chanakya acquired practical and experimental knowledge at Taxila. Chanakya's father Chanaka was also a teacher. He understood the importance of education and hence motivated his son towards the same. After completing his education at Taxila, Chanakya got appointed as a teacher there itself. He used to explain the principles of economics and philosophy with very pragmatic approach. Having been motivated towards education at a very early age, he understood the importance of the same quite well. That's why he had searched out Chandragupta Maurya at an early age and started imparting right education and training for preparing him to end the reign of cruel and immoral ruler Dhanananda of Pataliputra.

Devotion & Courage are Prerequisites for Knowledge

Knowledge is essential for human life. We all know and understand this. Children these days are admitted to schools very early in their childhood to enable them to acquire knowledge and build their path for success in life. But, if it were only knowledge required for success in the battlefield of life, how come so many persons who received very little of education or attended schools only for short periods grew to be eminent personalities? They became eminent as, in addition to regular studies, they also learnt other skills with same diligence. Coaching facilities are today available for cricket, football, acting, music, writing and many such skills. Coaching is definitely helpful, but only for those who learn with diligence. If a person is able to develop a sense of devotion, he may grow even from a very low level to a higher status in life and get the better of his peers.

Wyns Robert used to drive taxis until the age of 37. He had studied only up to 5th standard. He would wait for hours for passengers in front of hotels and airports. While waiting, he would often get lost in sweet dreams about having bungalow, cars and all other amenities of comfort some day. One day, while waiting, a passenger tried to wake him out of his daydream, "Please take me to my destination."

He said, "Well, how can I even think of having so much wealth? I don't possess any skills at all." The passenger replied with a smile, "Everybody possesses some or other skill. It has to be just refined with knowledge." Wyns was jolted by the words of the passenger.

When Wyns did not respond, the passenger clicked his fingers and said, "Hey, what happened? Are you lost dreaming of riches and fame?"

Wins came to senses on hearing this. He said, "Well, how can I even think of having so much wealth? I don't possess any skills at all."

The passenger replied with a smile, "Everybody possesses some or other skill. It has to be just refined with knowledge."

Wyns was jolted by the words of the passenger. He went to a bookstore one day and bought Webster Dictionary for 20 Pounds. He kept the dictionary on the front seat of his taxi. Out of curiosity, he opened the book when he was free and started reading the words on a page. He slowly started enjoying reading the same and tried to memorise each and every word in the dictionary. After finishing almost one-eighth of that dictionary, he started to easily comprehend all the things related to his studies. He would repeat those words while waiting at the taxi stand. Just like that, he developed curiosity in share market also. After getting to know the nitty-gritty of share market, he started investing in the same. His personal wealth started to grow and he launched a company with 19 taxis. Today, the world knows him as a billionaire.

Thus, Wyns Robert started with reading a dictionary at taxi stand to acquire knowledge and succeeded in realising his dreams.

Knowledge is the Breath of Life

The very fact that Chanakya always laid emphasis on knowledge is an indication of the importance of knowledge even today. He used to even say, "One should not stay at the place where it is not possible to acquire knowledge." Not only that, Chanakya was quite unhappy with the maternal uncle of Chandragupta Maurya as he was against his education and he felt that he would have to incur financial loss if Chandragupta left him. He even demanded money from Chanakya to cover up his loss. But, how could Chanakya have that much money? He was just a teacher - a teacher who tried to teach his students in any situation. He had noticed the potentials in Chandragupta Maurya and hence he had to agree to the demands of Chandragupta's uncle. Chanakya sold all his books and valuable scriptures to arrange funds and paid the same to Chandragupta's uncle. Being a teacher and highly devoted to knowledge, he had to even sell the other teachings in the form of those scriptures in order to continue the education of Chandragupta. Education is a fundamental right of every person. Chanakya even desired free education for every child to improve general level of education and to strengthen economic condition of the country.

Means of Acquiring Knowledge and Power of Words

Chanakya maintained that all the desires of a person who acquired knowledge get fulfilled. Knowledge destroys all the infirmities. Let's see which are the simple means of acquiring knowledge that may be accessible to everybody?

There are many ways of acquiring knowledge. Using them, even a common and illiterate individual may turn into a clever, educated and extraordinary personality.

- Keep a sharp eye all around.
- Pick your words carefully. According to Chanakya, a lethal iron arrow piercing the body may be pulled out but an arrow made of acerbic words can never be pulled out as the same pierces the heart. Hence, words should be used with great wisdom and rationality. Vitriolic words should never be spoken. The book '*The Words You Should Know*' by David Olsen contains 1200 words that everybody should know and also use.

The words of a language have their own beauty. Words take the shape of sentences and describe every incident. Words only create history, shape the present and lay foundation stones for the future. A person who acquires knowledge intensively becomes a scholar. He knows how to use words like magic. It's not only life that has magic but even the words contain magic. Every word has emotion, meaning, dimensions and some essence for its existence.

The words of a language have their own beauty. Words take the shape of sentences and describe every incident. Words only create history, shape the present and lay foundation stones for the future.

The word 'अनपढ़' means a person who is not literate or illiterate. If we pay attention to every vowel and consonant of the word, we find the word is made of

'अक्षरनपढ़'. The short form of 'अक्षरनपढ़' becomes 'अनपढ़'.

Similarly, the word 'राम' is found to have multiple meanings in Hindi, like -

Meaning Sentence

राम – name —राम स्कूल गया।

राम-राम – Salutation—राम-राम। सब ठीक है ना?

राम-राम-राम – Interjection—राम-राम-राम, क्या ज़माना आ गया है? कोई किसी की सुनता ही नहीं है।

If a person acquires education with full sincerity and devotion, he not only learns new things but he may also bring to light new words and ideas. Hence, Chanakya considered knowledge to be of paramount importance. An educated person can surmount all the challenges of life.

Life Domain-	**Knowledge**	**-Challenges**
⇔	○	⇔

Lessons from Chanakya

Just as a beautiful dhak (Butea) flower, despite being fragrant, is neither offered to deities nor able to attract anybody, an uneducated person, even if born in a respectable family and blessed with good appearance, is not able to earn respect in society. The grace and elegance of looks, beauty, riches, wealth, power, family and youth get better with intelligence and wisdom. In their absence, a person is like a dhak flower only. Knowledge is essential for a human being. All round development of a person is impossible in the absence of knowledge. With knowledge, a person may build his own ladder and reach the pinnacle of success.

❑

Woman Power

Acharya's Pearls of Wisdom

- *A woman is also like property, hence, protect her.*
- *A woman is six times more courageous than a man.*
- *A resolute woman can do things beyond imagination.*
- *People are generally unaware of the power of women.*

Woman Power is Unparalleled

There is no existence of family, society or country without women. A family, society or country gets its identity on the strength of its women only. But the women have been playing second fiddle since ages. Perhaps, emergence and existence of patriarchal societies may be the primary reason for the same, as otherwise, the power and personality of a woman have been described as incomparable everywhere right from the religious scriptures to Chanakya Niti. Women themselves also have proven the same from the very beginning, with their action and courage. If we look into the mythological era, we would find how goddess Durga slew the demons in different forms and brought relief to humanity. A wrong notion in respect of Ramayana and Mahabharata has been prevailing all along that women are the cause of all the battles. In fact, this notion does conceal a psychological belief that even a minor humiliation of a woman can cause havoc to the creation. Even a great man like Chanakya is found to be saying this in respect of women, "One cannot imagine what a woman can do if she gets determined. Irrespective of the environment in which they live, women who have the zeal to do something extraordinary would reach their goals even in adverse circumstances."

Women Have Been Ingenious in Different Activities Ever Since Ancient Times

Chanakya has described the power of women as unbound. Besides this, women have been more ingenious, as compared to men, in different activities since ancient times.

Even after going through the story of development of human kind, it can be understood easily that both men and women are entirely dependent on each other. Women are definitely not inferior to men; rather further exploration does reveal that women are more ingenious and gifted compared to men.

Yuval Noah Harari has provided a detailed description of development of humankind in his book *Sapiens*. He has also asserted that women possess excellent diplomacy and greater capability to look into matters from the point of view of others. As the development of humankind progressed, the society kept growing patriarchal and women were moulded into a shape limited by the desires of men. In ancient times, women, for generations, kept assuming that they were inferior to men. However, educated women later started raising their voice against those malpractices that were prevalent for ages and were impairing the rights of women. Even after going through the story of development of humankind, it can be understood easily that both men and women are entirely dependent on each other. Women are definitely not inferior to men; rather further exploration does reveal that women are more ingenious and gifted compared to men. This has been proven by Indian women as well as women around the world.

Women Power in Indian Army, Navy and Air Force

Indian Army: By successfully completing the 1100 km bike expedition in 14 days with a bike weighing 194 kg, traversing the terrain against icy winds at a height of 18605 ft. with temperature hovering around -30° C, Major K Renuka of Indian Army has proven that no adverse condition can become an obstacle in your path if you have courage and confidence. She was the leader of the 'Himalayan Heights Bike Expedition' team. In coordination with Royal Enfield, the Indian Army had flagged off this expedition on 7 April 2019 from Leh to celebrate 20th Kargil Victory Diwas and to pay homage to the martyrs. This was a very difficult route and Major K Renuka made the entire country proud by completing the same successfully on a heavy bike.

After getting down from the aircraft, she celebrated her feat with Indian flag in her hands and said, "I am so honoured and grateful that I could do this for my country and for women everywhere. Flying alone in a little plane, with the light blue sky above and the dark blue sea below was quite a thrilling experience."

Similarly, black-belt holder Dr Seema Rao is currently the only female commando trainer of India. She has already trained 20,000 male soldiers till date.

Indian Navy: Six woman officers from Indian Navy - Lt Commander Vartika Joshi, Lt Commander Pratibha Jamwal, Lt Commander Swati P., Lieutenant Aishwarya Boddapati, Lieutenant S. Vijaya Devi and Lieutenant Payal Gupta created history by successfully completing an expedition on 55 ft. I.N.S. Tarini in eight months i.e.254 days. They covered a distance of 21,600 nautical miles during this expedition and crossed the equator, four continents and three oceans twice.

Indian Air Force: 23-year-old Aarohi Pandit of Mumbai has flown across Atlantic Ocean in a light sport aircraft. She is the first woman pilot not only in India but also in the world to accomplish this. She flew in a single engine Sinus-912 light sport aircraft named ‘Mahi’. The weight of this aircraft is only 400 kg, even less than a Bullet motorcycle. Aarohi landed at Iqaluit Airport in Canada on 14 May 2019 after covering around 3000 km distance . After getting down from the aircraft, she celebrated her feat with Indian national flag in her hands and said, “I am so honoured and grateful that I could do this for my country and for women everywhere. Flying alone in a little plane, with the light blue sky above and the dark blue sea below was quite a thrilling experience.”

Thus, woman officers from all the three armed forces of India have proven by demonstrating their strength and diligence that only courage and zest are required to touch the heights of success. For a determined and self-confident person, ‘gender’ makes no difference for attaining a goal.

Power of an Indian Mother

This is a myth that women busy in managing households and taking care of their children are unable to carve out their personal identities. This myth has been busted completely by Mangte Chungneijang Mary Kom i.e. M. C. Mary Kom. She got married to K. Onkholer Kom in the year 2005. They have three children now. While still parenting her children, M. C. Mary Kom stunned the entire world by claiming her 6th World Championship title on 24 November 2018 in 10th AIBA Women's World Boxing Championship event. Today, Mary Kom has everything - unnumbered awards, fame and money her credit. She has been able to reinforce the impression, not only in the Indian society rather in the entire world, that women, supported wholeheartedly by fellow men, may conquer the world.

Chanakya had emphasised women empowerment 2400 years ago itself. Not only this, he had even given a lesson on this to Chandragupta who had established Maurya Dynasty at that time. Chandragupta Maurya could become immortal in history only because of his guru Chanakya.

Chandragupta Maurya Realises the Importance of Women Empowerment

Chanakya had emphasised women empowerment 2400 years ago itself. Not only this, he had even given a lesson on this to Chandragupta who established Maurya Dynasty at that time. Chandragupta Maurya could become immortal in history only because of his guru Chanakya. One day, while discussing some state affairs with Chandragupta Maurya, Chanakya said, "We should give thought to the condition of women."

"Why Acharya, what is the matter? Women are very safe here," said Chandragupta.

Acharya explained, "There is no doubt that the condition of women is quite good here, but I wish to make the same still better."

"In what way?" asked Chandragupta, looking a bit confused.

"I want every married woman to feel that she also has a separate identity and she has the capacity to take decision. Hence, women should be involved in all activities. Occasionally, we may even confer with them on state affairs and listen to their suggestions and complaints patiently. Many a time, even deep meanings may be concealed in the same."

Surprised over Acharya Chanakya's idea, Chandragupta responded, "Acharya, I am not able to understand anything. After all, where is the need to involve women in state affairs?"

"Maharaja, you still need to learn a lot," replied Chanakya.

As suggested by Chanakya, Chandragupta Maurya conferred with Raja Mata and his wife that day on some serious issues of the state and he realised that both of them felt quite happy and had presented their views quite sagaciously. He said to Chanakya, "Acharya, your policy has been quite effective. Both the ladies were very happy."

Chanakya said, "I am still not entirely happy with the condition of women. They have unlimited power. It's a complete myth that they can only do cooking. They have their own innate mind and intelligence. Hence, you keep on taking help from your mother and your wife on state affairs. The visual sense of a woman is quite sharp and inside her, there is always present a sixth sense that gets awakened at the slightest sign of danger. Women only are the surest means to take the country towards progress."

Chanakya said, "I am still not entirely happy with the condition of women. They have unlimited power. It's a complete myth that they can only do cooking. They have their own innate mind and intelligence. Hence, you keep on taking help from your mother and your wife on state affairs. The visual sense of a woman is quite sharp and inside her, there is always present a sixth sense that gets awakened at the slightest sign of danger. Women only are the surest means to take the country towards progress."

Chandragupta Maurya understood the seriousness of Chanakya's idea and started to cooperate with him in his quest for women empowerment.

Thus, Chanakya had, from the very beginning, recognised the intricacies of unlimited power of women. Today, women in India, by touching the sky on the strength of their abilities, wisdom and achievements, have also proven that women ably supported by fellow men can even remove mountains from their path.

Give a woman the respect she deserves. Chanakya had also given instructions for severe punishment for misbehaviour with women. He would say, "If a person forcibly kills a woman, kidnaps a woman by force, disfigures the face of a woman or commits burglary by threatening to kill her, that culprit should be crucified."

Encourage Women-Power

- Pay attention to upbringing of girls. Celebrate their birth. The birth of a girl child is celebrated in Piplantri village of Rajasthan by planting 111 saplings. The birth of a girl child should be celebrated in a similar way everywhere.
- Get rid of the notion that a woman is an alien property. Instead, try to develop a mentality that a woman is a source of light for not one but two houses. If her personality is developed from the very childhood, she would be capable of illumining two houses, else it would not take much time for that source of light to get extinguished.
- Give a woman the respect she deserves. Chanakya had also given instructions for severe punishment for misbehaviour with women. He would say, "If a person forcibly kills a woman, kidnaps a woman by force, disfigures the face of a woman or commits burglary by threatening to kill her, that culprit should be crucified."
- Always respect your daughter, sister, wife and mother in your house and try to develop their talents.
- Do not indulge in female foeticide at any cost. Slaughter, whether that of a foetus or a creature, is a heinous crime.

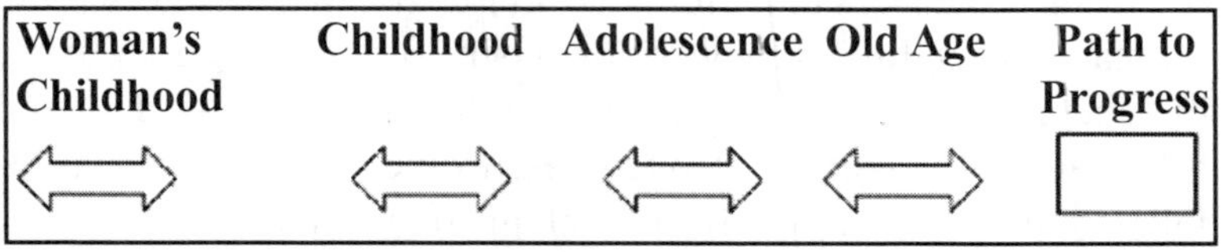

Woman's Childhood	**Childhood**	**Adolescence**	**Old Age**	**Path to Progress**
⇔	⇔	⇔	⇔	☐

Lessons from Chanakya

Compared to men, women possess higher aptitude for work in all areas. In this regard, Chanakya considers women not equal to but much above of men. Explaining this in his Niti, he says, "Women have hunger two-fold, shyness four-fold, courage six-fold and lust eight-fold compared to men."

Women have mental ability many times more than that of men. Hence, they are able to simultaneously handle multiple activities very efficiently and achieve success. A woman at the same time attends to her job, takes care of her children, nurses aged parents, handles household chores and also efficiently discharges her financial and official duties. Hence, while reading this book, every woman should feel pride in being incarnated on this earth as a woman. She is a creator and also the architect of this universe. She may remain confined out of shyness and at the same time, may also fearlessly destroy the enemy when such a need arises.

❑

Married Life

Acharya's Pearls of Wisdom

- *The pain of separation from wife is unbearable.*
- *One should be neither too close nor too far from a king, a fire, a guru and a woman.*
- *People nurturing love in their hearts have to suffer grief only.*

Types of Marriages

Chanakya alias Kautilya has classified marriages into 8 types. They are as following:

1. Brahmya Marriage
2. Prajapatya Marriage
3. Aarsha Marriage

4. Daiva Marriage
5. Gandharva Marriage
6. Asura Marriage
7. Rakshasa Marriage
8. Paisacha Marriage

All these 8 types of marriages have been taking place ever since mythological era. First four types of marriages are considered lawful and sacred as they are performed with the consent of the families concerned. In ancient times, when evolution of humankind was still in infancy, there was neither any society nor any system. Some evolutionist psychologists believe that prehistoric food hunter groups did not have husband-wife centric families and they lived in communities devoid of monogamy and parentage.

Many people turn psychotic after separation while many others are hurt to the extent that they even commit suicide. Hence, there is a need for improvement in the institution of marriage as is existing today. These days, not only the groom but the bride also is generally educated and financially independent. In such a situation, the bride is not ready to tolerate misbehaviour, maltreatment and violence and she starts protesting against the same quite vehemently.

Bonding of Marriage

Marriage is a bond that binds husband and wife with each other for many lives. They start sharing their happiness and sorrow. If marriage is successful, both husband and wife move ahead with their personal growth in the society. However, if marriage unfortunately goes awry, it creates many issues in the society. Marriages in the Indian society have been generally taking place with the consent of parents and usually last forever. However, the situation today is not the same. A question mark lingers on the institution of marriage in the modern society. If the views of bride's side and groom's side do not match properly, the relationship turns into a black spot instead of an everlasting sweet bonding. Breaking of a relationship is painful. Many people turn psychotic after separation while many others are hurt to the extent that they even end their life by committing suicide. Hence, there is a need for improvement in the institution of marriage as existing today. These days, not only the groom but the bride also is generally educated and financially independent. In such a situation, the bride is not ready to tolerate misbehaviour, maltreatment and violence and she starts protesting against the same quite vehemently. When a silent voice becomes vociferous, it is natural for the sentinels of relationship to get startled. Psychologists have, after studying cognitive and hormone related systems of males and females, confirmed that males have more of aggressive and violent tendencies. Hence, because of their male chauvinism, they indulge in violent behaviour with women. In the current scenario, women are not ready to tolerate violent behaviour.

Chanakya believes that joys and sorrows of a bride and her groom become common for both after marriage and they should lead their life striking a balance with love and affection towards each other. A person develops a family after marriage and then he gets enmeshed in greed and attachment. While family provides support to a person, the same becomes a reason for grief also. Chanakya says, "He who is too attached to his family does have to face fear and anxiety."

Chanakya believes that extraordinarily intelligent, clever and brilliant people do not marry, as they prefer to choose their goals and actions as their life companions and life partners. It may be correct to some extent to say that every person should definitely get married as the same provides him security and stability but at the same time, this also is true that if a person remains fully dedicated to his goal and karma, they become his life companions.

Many a time, the rise and fall of a person depends on his marriage. After raising a family, this becomes all the more necessary for the husband and the wife to take care of each other as well as of their family. A person has to sacrifice his desires for fulfilling the needs of his family.

Marriage An Obstacle

A society consists of people and man also is a social animal. However, those people who are extraordinarily brilliant are often able to progress only when they diligently concentrate on their work all alone. Many a time, company of other people or a crowd takes such a person away from his goal. Chanakya also makes the same point, "If you need to do meditation, do it alone." Meditation here does not mean pooja rituals alone, instead it refers to the battle of life. If two partners who understand the feelings of each other and help each other fight this battle of life, a marriage becomes the greatest blessing of life. On the other hand, if the condition the other way round, it does not take much time for that marriage to become a bane. Chanakya believes that extraordinarily intelligent, clever and brilliant people do not marry, as they prefer to choose their goals and actions as their life companions and life partners. It may be correct to some extent to say that every person should definitely get married as the same provides him security and stability but at the same time, this also is true that if a person remains fully dedicated to his goal and karma, that goal and karma become his life companions. Chanakya himself is a glaring example of the same. He remained unmarried for his entire life. He dedicated his entire life to welfare of this country and to make India a prosperous nation.

Mystery of Chanakya's Bachelorhood

Once, one of Chanakya's childhood friends came to see him. He had already seen his brilliance and vigour in his childhood itself and he firmly believed that Chanakya was different from the other common people. That friend had already got married and his family included his parents, his modest wife and a child. After narrating everything about himself, the friend said, "Vishnu, I know that you have come to this world with some specific purpose and you would not stop until you achieve the same."

Chanakya smiled softly over his friend's words and tried to change the topic. But his friend also was not ready to quit. He said, "I just have to know the mystery of your remaining unmarried."

"I am not against marriage, but it is not made for me."

"Yes, I want to transform India into a powerful nation and I would like to install a ruler here whose first priority is the welfare of common people," responded Chanakya.

His friend said, "That's okay. It's not a difficult target for you. You are resolute and you can do anything. You just tell me why you did not get married? Any woman would have admired her fate for being your wife."

Chanakya smiled softly over his friend's words and tried to change the topic. But his friend also was hell bent on knowing the fact. He said, "I just have to know the mystery of your remaining unmarried."

"I am not against marriage, but it is not made for me."

"Why Vishnu?" His friend was surprised.

"Because I am already married," clarified Chanakya.

"What are you talking?" The friend's jaw dropped in surprise, "When and with whom did you marry?"

"I am already wedded to the goal of nation building and the welfare of my people."

His friend was also not ready to quit. He said, "This you could have done even after marriage."

Chanakya was still smiling softly. He looked towards his friend and said, "You are correct. I could have done this even after marriage. But I did not want to lose sight of my point of focus. Marriage is a huge responsibility and many a time, a person has to sacrifice many things for the same. If you wed a wrong partner, your problems are going to increase only. A person can remain focussed on only one point. If his attention is diverted to multiple issues, he would not be able to attain any of his objectives, be it a goal or an art or a service to his motherland."

These words made his friend realise that Vishnu had a very sharp mind and was taking every step deliberately. He never raised this point again with Chanakya after this.

Anybody Can Be Your Life Partner

In the present context, the meaning of life partner is not limited to husband or wife only. Humankind is in a quite developed stage today. Market is full of products that enable a person to get rid of his loneliness. If a person still feels lonely, he may find a beautiful way out by means of creations. Otherwise also, loneliness is the best friend of a person. Best of the creations are achieved in loneliness only. It's only in loneliness that a person reaches the pinnacle of meditation. Loneliness only establishes concentration.

A person may choose anything like books, music, dance, science, writing or painting as his life partner. If you make books, art or science your life partner, you are never alone as they all are constantly growing and keep providing fresh ideas every day. A mind that is guarded by creativity is always free from tension and problems.

A person may choose anything like books, music, dance, science, writing or painting as his life partner. If you make books, art or science your life partner, you are never alone as they are all constantly growing and keep providing fresh ideas every day. A mind that is guarded by creativity is always free from tension and problems.

Think Before You Enter Into Wedlock

Do not get disheartened even if you are unmarried or deserted or widow or widower, rather make your hobbies your companions. Believe me, your hobbies would stand by you for the whole life and even after life. If a person is frustrated with his spouse and is unable to decide on separation, his life turns into an ulcer and he is compelled to live and die with the same.

Many people get married just to satisfy the wishes of their families and keep agonising later, to get out of this bondage to satisfy their hobbies and give direction to their lives. They finally liberate themselves and set out to attain their goals. Gautam Buddha did the same. He was married to Yashodhara but after getting estranged from his own life, he left his young wife and his son Rahul sleeping and set out in search of knowledge. Of course, Gautam Buddha attained nirvana with the help of knowledge but the lives of Yashodhara and Rahul turned into tragedies. Hence, it's appropriate to enter into wedlock only after adequate thinking. Marriage is a huge responsibility. This requires a life partner to take care of offspring and aged parents besides his or her spouse. This responsibility lies not only with the bride but also with the groom. Many a time, the bride is the only child of her parents and in that case, lives of her aged parents become quite miserable after her marriage. The husband should demonstrate prudence in such a case and accept the responsibility of taking care of them also. In real sense, this is the meaning of being life partners where both of them share their joys and sorrows for entire life.

Live Your Life to the Fullest

Do not get disheartened even if you are unmarried or deserted or widow or widower, rather make your hobbies your companions. Believe me, your hobbies would stand by you for the whole life and even after life. If a person is frustrated with his spouse and is unable to decide on separation, his life turns into an ulcer and he is compelled to live and die with the same. When the spouse is not as per one's liking, is always indulging in mistreatment and, instead of providing support, keeps on encouraging conflicts, it becomes quite difficult to survive. Every object or situation or relationship has both positives and negatives. Hence, even if you do not have that object or relationship or situation, just make your hobbies your life partner instead of getting dejected and learn to live your life to the fullest. Life would become quite wonderful. Just remember, life is meant to be enjoyed, not endured!

Man-Woman	**Life-Partners**	**Books/ Art/ Science**	**Growth**
☺☺	⇔	☼	⇔

Lessons from Chanakya

If a person is extraordinarily brilliant and he wants to use his brilliance for the benefit of his society and country, he should better make his talent, hobbies and style of work themselves as his companions for life.

Chanakya considers marriage a very important step in the life of a person. This step must be taken with care or else both the bride and the groom may have to pay the price for the same. Before deciding on a marital relationship, people should collect accurate information with regard to character, education and families of the bride and the groom. This is a relationship for life. If this relationship is established between suitable families and persons, the life becomes enjoyable else it does not take much time for the life to turn into a hell. Many a time, it's the prudence of the bride and the groom that makes the journey of life easy and makes living great. If a person is extraordinarily brilliant and he wants to use his brilliance for the benefit of his society and country, he should better make his talent, hobbies and style of work themselves as his companions for life.

❑

Qualities of Birds and Animals

Acharya's Pearls of Wisdom

- *Humans should embrace one quality each from lion and heron, three from donkey, four from cock, five from crow and six from dog.*
- *The four qualities of cocks - waking up on time, being always ready for fight, sharing with kith and kin judiciously and taking care of one's companion - are worth emulating.*
- *The qualities like penchant for hoarding and avoiding lethargy should be picked up from a crow.*
- *Six qualities of dogs viz. capacity to over-eat, being content with little in the time of scarcity, sleeping well, being alert even when sleeping, loyalty and fighting the enemy valiantly should be embraced.*
- *Working tirelessly, not worrying about weather conditions, patience and contentment - these are the your qualities of a donkey that should be imbibed.*

Human Mind

Humans are considered to be the most intelligent creature of this living world. A human is the only creature who can think and speak and then work according to what he has thought and spoken or even act contrary to the same. In other words, he has the capacity to act even without thinking and expressing. God has provided humans with qualities that can help him even touch the sky. Everybody is equal at the time of birth unless there is some congenital deformity in him. Though, even people with congenital issues, if blessed with courage and resolve, move ahead in their lives without bothering about their physical or mental deformities and they often create history. With their great deeds and tremendous courage, they draw a thin golden line as a guiding beacon for the coming generations to tread along the same and build their golden castles. A person may, by awakening his potentials and practising regularly, make his mind extremely strong.

Intelligence of Other Creatures

Man is an intelligent creature but that does not mean at all that he just does not have to find out or learn anything from others. Even the smallest of things or creatures of this nature and the living world may teach great lessons to humankind. Chanakya has understood those very minutiae and merits of the creatures. He even exhorts we, humans to learn from them.

Industriousness of Ants

Insects have great relevance in the life of a human. Ant is a small creature. Its size is normally between 2mm and 7mm. Its brain consists of very large number of cells and is considered to be quite sharp. Ants, with their lifestyle, convey that life should be always lived with positive thoughts and one should not get afraid of struggle. An ant possesses the capacity to lift almost 20 times its own weight and knows how to successfully come out of the storm. Ants are compassionate and they take care of their fellow ants, even to the extent of arranging food for them. Not only that, ants also play an important role in our ecological system. They recycle the nutrients of soil and help in growth and development of seeds.

An ant possesses the capacity to lift almost 20 times its own weight and knows how to successfully come out of the storm. Ants are compassionate and they take care of their fellow ants, even to the extent of arranging food for them. Not only that, ants also play an important part in our ecological system. They recycle the nutrients of soil and help in growth and development of seeds.

Short But Amazing Life of Butterflies

Butterflies are very beautiful and attractive creatures. Their lifespan is very short. Within that short lifespan, these butterflies, with their colourful wings, keep hovering over colourful flowers and share happiness with the humans as well as with the Nature. This way, they convey the message that this life, whether short or long, should be lived with smile. The birth of a butterfly is quite a struggle and the most interesting part of its life is that a tiny caterpillar, also known as larva, hatches from its egg. This grows eating leaves of plants and develops an exoskeleton around its body. This is the form of a pupa. The shell around this pupa is quite hard. A beautiful butterfly actually comes out into this world by breaking this shell. The butterfly has to risk its life while breaking this shell, but once it's out, it is free to move around in the open sky. One of the peculiar facts about the life of a butterfly is that if it is provided any help during the process of coming out of the shell after pupa is formed, it gets debilitated and dies within a short time. Thus, its lovely life conveys a message that a person is ready to live his life only when he comes out of the shell of struggles and pains all by himself.

Shrewdness and Agility of Crows

Chanakya had a sharp mind since his very childhood. Besides recognising the strong and weak points of enemies, friends, women and men, he was able to easily identify the strong and weak elements of birds and animals also. He had also explored the strong points of crows very minutely. Crow is a small bird but there is no comparison to its intelligence.

Chanakya had a sharp mind since his very childhood. Besides recognising the strong and weak points of enemies, friends, women and men, he was able to easily identify the strong and weak elements of birds and animals also. He had also explored the strong points of crows very minutely. Crow is a small bird but there is no comparison to its intelligence. A common crow generally lives for 15 to 30 years. Chanakya exhorts people to imbibe some of its qualities. The crow impresses not only with its ability to resolve its problems but also with its amazing communication skills. It's such a creature that knows very well how to come out of any trouble. Lethargy can never take over a crow. It remains alert even when it nears its old age. Crows go looking for food as per weather conditions and even store the same for rainy days. People generally don't like crows but crow is a social creature. Its memory is quite sharp and it can remember a human face for life. The life of a crow is limited to only eating and wandering about in the sky. Despite that, it does neither idle nor likes people who keep idling.

Lethargy is a very bad habit of humans. One should abstain from making the same his habit. The tendency of lethargy even worsens the life of a clever and talented person. On the other hand, even a person with average intelligence may reach the heights of success if he is not lethargic and is constantly focusing on his work.

Simplicity and Hard Work of a Donkey

Humans usually use the word 'donkey' to refer to a fool or a naive person or their enemies. Humans are also peculiar in a sense. If a person is addressed as 'donkey', he gets angry whereas the fact is that donkey, a member of the horse family, keeps working tirelessly. It can lift many times its own weight and remains content and patient in all situations. In real life, many people do not work even 10% of the amount of hard work that a donkey puts in.

Humans usually use the word 'donkey' to refer to a fool or a naive person or their enemies. Humans are also peculiar in a sense. If a person is addressed as 'donkey', he gets angry whereas the fact is that donkey, a member of the horse family, keeps working tirelessly. It can lift many times its own weight and remains content and patient in all situations. In real life, many people do not work even 10% of the amount of hard work that a donkey puts in. Still they feel offended when addressed as a donkey. This is going on for ages. Otherwise, if you ponder over the issue, you would find that if people emulate donkeys to be simple, balanced and hard-working, not only their personal growth but also economic, social and political growth of the country would start showing upward trend. The most astute diplomat Chanakya studied the minutiae and qualities of every object right from a donkey and advised everybody to adopt them. He transformed his disciple Chandragupta from a common person to an extraordinary ruler. Along with the regular lessons, he also provided practical aspects of all his teachings to Chandragupta Maurya. He even encouraged Chandragupta to learn from birds and animals.

In modern times, both contentment and patience are disappearing from the human world. That is the reason that the incidents of crime, corruption and violence have been on the rise these days. Prevalence of discontent among people is making trivial matters exploding into major and terrible disputes. These disputes even result in violence and unnecessary loss of lives.

Develop Trustworthiness as That of a Dog

Man is a creature that can change its nature based on circumstances. On the other hand, dog is a very honest and loyal animal. It maintains its faithfulness till its last breath. A dog may become aware of the frame of mind of a person just by looking into his eyes. This is beyond one's understanding as humans have unreasonably classified the word 'dog' itself as that referring to indecency.

Dogbelongs to the wolf family. This is the main domestic animal for humans. Today, it has become an important part of families and human lives. The receptiveness and hearing ability of a dog are quite incredible. Dogs can hear sounds as high as 35000 Hz whereas an average adult human can hear sounds only up to 20000 Hz. Today, dogs are not only protecting people in their homes but are also playing important roles in military warfare. Dogs are specially trained for security purpose. Man is a creature that can change its nature based on circumstances. On the other hand, dog is a very honest and loyal animal. It maintains its faithfulness till its last breath. A dog may become aware of the frame of mind of a person just by looking into his eyes. This is beyond one's understanding as humans have unreasonably classified the word 'dog' itself as that referring to indecency. Chanakya, on the other hand, emphasises that if people learn from dogs and imbibe their qualities, they may take their lives to the pinnacle of success. Plenty of true stories are available everywhere depicting the loyalty of dogs. It's surprising to note that while many of those stories are old, there are many such stories of recent times also. That shows that even today, dogs are as trustworthy, loyal and honest as they were centuries ago, whereas a person does not take even seconds to change his colours like a chameleon depending on the circumstances. Chanakya, with his skills, profundity and work ethics, not only changed the history of India but also enriched the entire world with his teachings, writings and character. Today, countries with their policies incorporating those very principles of economics propounded by Chanakya, though in moderated forms, are achieving great results. If a person understands Chanakya's principles and the wisdom hidden in them and practises them in his life and assimilates a mixture of some good qualities of birds and animals into his personality, the aroma of his personality would fill the atmosphere all around him like that of sandalwood and keep humming the melody of his fame.

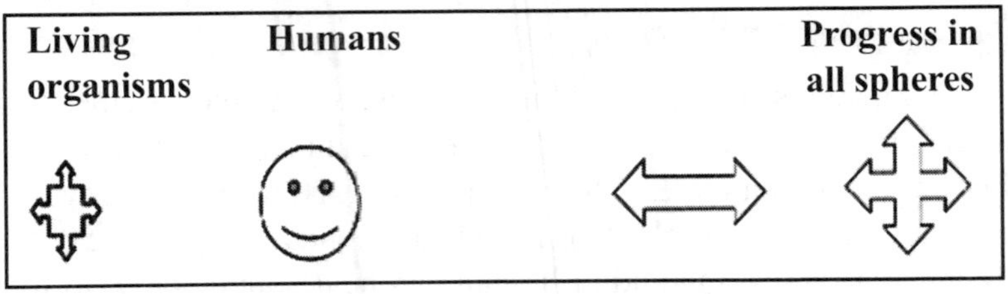

Living organisms	**Humans**		**Progress in all spheres**
✥	☺	⇔	✥

Lessons from Chanakya

Chanakya spent his entire life understanding the activities and characteristics of humans and other creatures and acquiring knowledge out of the same. He has exhorted people to take lessons not only from humans but also from birds and animals. Ants, butterflies, crows, donkeys and dogs are creatures in the animal kingdom that are not only very useful for humans but whose lives offer great emulable examples for people in this world.

❑

Child Development from the Viewpoint of Chanakya

Acharya's Pearls of Wisdom

- *A potter uses a lump or clay rotating on a wheel to form a beautiful shape of a utensil, sometimes tapping that clay lump, sometimes caressing the same and sometimes beating it. Once ready, the same utensil attracts people with its beauty. Parents should nurture their clay-like children just like that potter.*
- *A father should bring up his child with love up to the age of 5 years. After that, he should be strict with the child for next 10 years. Once the child is 16 years old, he should be treated as a friend.*

Confusion in the Mind of a Child

Thousands of years back, Chanakya had studied minutely the lives of children, women, men, rulers, soldiers, gurus and even birds and animals. This was the reason that he was able to transform a common boy like Chandragupta into an extraordinary emperor of India. Childhood is the golden period of the life of a person. This is the age when he finds magic exciting and tries to look for magic in everything. Everything excites him right from colourful butterflies, coloured flowers and beautiful flowing streams of rivers to the sun rising from the hills. A magician uses prestidigitation to enthral children. When 25 December approaches, all children right from the age of three years to six years, impatiently wait for Santa Claus and wish for their favourite gifts. Next day, when they find their gifts on their beds or in some corners of their houses, the happiness and glow on their faces look all the more brightened with the rays of the sun. Everything in the stories - lives of the angels, fulfilment of all desires and reaching pinnacle of success - look real and every child craves to achieve the same kind of success in his life, but as he grows, the confusion in his tender mind keeps getting more chaotic. He would have had a glimpse of beautiful and exciting life in those stories and books, but in real life, scolding of his parents, rebuke from his teachers and ridicule by his friends hurt him very much. All these things make a tender mind so confused that the child often gets discomposed and many a time, even gets derailed from his path of development.

Chanakya emphasises on presentation of powerful pictorials before children in order to eliminate confusion from their minds. One picture is more powerful than hundred words!

Some Wrong Pictures of Childhood

- Some parents still believe in beating children as they had received beating in their childhood from their parents. Their own beating had created an impression in their minds that children could be disciplined only by beating.

- Indecent behaviour of some men with women also has links with wrong experiences during their childhood. They would have seen their fathers indulging in physical abuse and indecent behaviour with their mothers. Such pictures get engrained in their subconscious minds. Most of the violent incidents taking place against women have the same background.

Some parents still believe in beating children as they had received beating in their childhood from their parents. Their own beating had created an impression in their minds that children could be disciplined only by beating.

- India is a patriarchal country. Hence, even today, most of the men consider themselves all-powerful. After marriage, instead of treating their wives as equal partners for life, they treat them as subordinate to themselves and do not give any importance to their opinions, desires and activities. As a result, incidents of divorce, suicide, etc. are becoming quite common these days. Mistreating one's wife or ignoring the views of women or not caring for their condition are the things that a child learns right in his childhood.
- Quite often, in order to avoid a guest, parents ask their child to tell the guest that they are not at home or that they are busy in some urgent work. The child does convey to the guest as instructed by his parents but gets this engrained in his subconscious mind that such kind of lies are not unethical. He also repeats the same when he is adult.
- Parents usually reprimand their children on securing low scores in their examinations and even entice them with expensive gifts for scoring well. Once grown up, those children also use the same gimmicks with their children. Not only this, the children start to believe that they can get expensive gifts only when they fulfil the expectations of others. This is a very wrong concept.

Chanakya was a great scholar. He studied not only the scriptures but also the people. He used to say, "Good nature and good behaviour are the main qualities of a human being." All the riches, relatives and his life are of no use to a person who loses his morality. Hence, development of good nature and good behaviour in a person must start in the childhood itself.

Chanakya was a great scholar. He studied not only the scriptures but also the people. He used to say, "Good nature and good behaviour are the main qualities of a human being." All the riches, relatives and his life are of no use to a person who loses his morality. Hence, development of good nature and good behaviour in a person must start in his childhood itself. Even if parents have gone through painful lives, they should still try to idealise themselves in front of their children.

Parents are the Child's First Role Models

Whatever be the nature and behaviour of his parents, they are role models for a child. Parents are the first school in the lives of their children. The first time a baby opens its eyes, it finds the parents as its protectors and tries to emulate them as it grows. A child is often called monkey for his habit of imitating. Monkeys are expert in imitating. This way, a child imbibes all the habits and manners as per the ambience and environment. He assimilates his parents' work habits, knowledge, etc. A child considers his parents the best in all respects. This gets engrained in his mind that all the things that his parents do are correct, and he treats even improper behaviours of his parents as right. Hence, parents should always behave as role models in front of their child. People are required to forgo many of their desires to become good parents. Chanakya considers Grihastha stage of life very important and full of responsibilities and advises that those responsibilities should be fulfilled with complete honesty and integrity. The status of parents has been treated even above that of guru or God only because they are expected to infuse the best of morals into their children even if that costs everything in their own lives.

Practical Lessons Essential

In addition to school education and books, practical lessons are also quite essential for children. They should be imparted such practical lessons from time to time. Chanakya did not forget to often pass on practical knowledge to his disciples while attending to daily routines. He had imparted practical lessons to Chandragupta over and over again. Chandragupta Maurya was extremely talented.

In addition to school education and books, practical lessons are also quite essential for children. They should be imparted such practical lessons from time to time. Chanakya did not forget to often pass on practical knowledge to his disciples while attending to daily routines. He had imparted practical lessons to Chandragupta over and over again. Chandragupta Maurya was extremely talented and he also knew that Chanakya liked him very much. He would often make the mistake of considering himself accomplished with all the good qualities in this world and treat even his hasty decisions as appropriate. One day, Chandragupta chalked out a strategy to launch assault on his enemies. As per this strategy, he planned to make a direct attack on the enemy army. When Chanakya came to know of the same, he decided to pass on a practical lesson to him. He invited Chandragupta for dinner that night and got some rice cooked for him. Chandragupta was served hot rice in a plate. Just as he started to eat, Chanakya said, “Wait!”

He pointed towards the plate and said, “Assume this to be the battlefield and the rice to be enemy battalion.”

Chandragupta understood that he was going to get some practical lesson. He replied, “Yes Guruji, I am assuming this rice to be enemy army and this plate to be enemy’s fort.”

"Good! Now tell me where do you expect the enemy king to be there?"

Chandragupta thought over the same for sometime and responded, "Guruji, as per my understanding, the enemy king should be in the middle of the plate."

"Why?" Chanakya asked.

"Because that provides him protection from all sides."

Chanakya smiled at his response and said, "Very good! So you can easily win the battle by killing the king?"

"Yes Guruji! That's why I plan to attack the king directly and defeat him."

Chanakya looked a bit apprehensive and said, "Show me execution of your strategy in this plate."

On hearing this, Chandragupta immediately placed his hand in the middle of rice. As the rice was very hot, he felt his fingers burning and he pulled back his hand with a scream.

Observing this, Chanakya asked, "Do you really feel it would be easy to make a direct assault on the king protected from all sides in his territory?"

Chandragupta realised his mistake. He said, "Acharya, what should I do in such a situation?"

"In such a situation, you should destroy the army from its sides. It is generally weak at its boundaries and can be easily overpowered. Thus, instead of making a direct assault on a well protected kingdom, its perimeter should be attacked."

Chandragupta tried to feel the rice at the sides of the plate and found them to be comparatively less hot. He could easily eat the rice from that area. He went on eating that way and by the time he reached the middle of the plate, the rice there also had turned cold.

This practical common sense taught Chandragupta an important lesson in martial arts. Chandragupta greeted guru Chanakya and thanked him for making him understand so easily the ways to take on enemies.

This way, Chanakya used to pass on a lot of practical wisdom to Chandragupta through daily routine jobs, even during meals. All round growth of a child can be accomplished only if he is also provided practical knowledge.

It's Essential to Take Care of a Child in all Earnestness

When both the parents are working, they are not able to pay proper attention to their child. The child, in such a case, feels alienated. Many a time, just to get his parents' attention, he indulges in unruly behaviour and naughty acts and even gets involved in scuffles at his school just hoping that the matter reaches his parents and he gets their attention.

When both the parents are working, they are not able to pay proper attention to their child. The child, in such a case, feels alienated. Many a time, just to get his parents' attention, he indulges in unruly behaviour and naughty tricks and even gets involved in scuffles at his school just hoping that the matter reaches his parents and he gets their attention. It's prime responsibility of the parents not to loose attention from their children even if they are too busy. This problem may be resolved just by managing time with little prudence and intelligence.

- Have at least one meal of the day with your child.
- Enquire how he spent the day and whether anything special happened at his school on the day. This should be done everyday without fail, even if it is limited to 5 or 10 minutes.
- Even if the child is going for tuition, do check his notebooks once a day. This would make the child feel that he is being cared for.
- Inculcate in your child a habit of book reading at night.

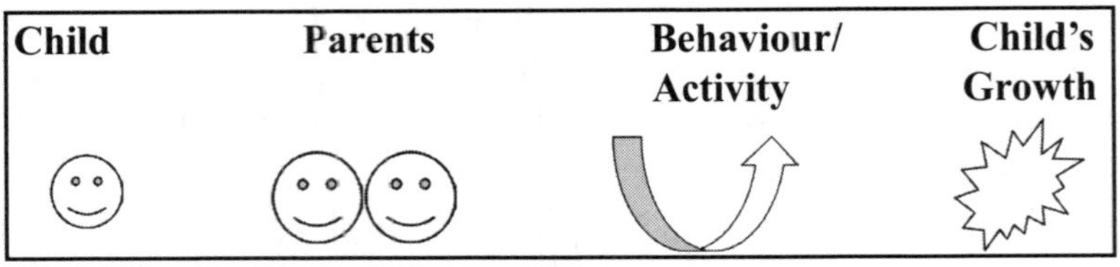

Child	Parents	Behaviour/ Activity	Child's Growth

Lessons from Chanakya

Chanakya held education to be essential for everybody. He believed childhood to be very innocent. A child always follows his parents. Hence, every parent should always try to profess the path of honesty, non-violence, love and kindness in front of their children. This is possible only when the parents themselves also follow the same path. Parents may raise their children to be good citizens only when they have positive approach and are optimistic about them. They should never, even by mistake, exhibit any inappropriate behaviour involving violence, falsehood and inactivity in front of their children. Children are the leaders of tomorrow. In order to ensure a bright future for the country, it is essential that children today are provided exciting surroundings and positive environment.

❑

Appreciate Your Prosperity, Donate Liberally

Acharya's Pearls of Wisdom

- *The person, who, despite being poor, is charitable, attains a place even higher than the heaven.*
- *Charitable giving to a right receiver comes back to the giver thousand times multiplied.*
- *Charity never goes waste. Ten times of the same comes back as reward.*
- *To keep his erudition meaningful, every human being should practise charitable giving as per his capacity. This benefits him in this world as well as in the other world.*

Charity Does Not Diminish Wealth

Chanakya had gone through good, bad and very bad phases in his life. Every stage and struggle of his life had made him very practical. He would often see his mother giving things to saints and sages. One day when his mother was offering to a needy man, Chanakya raised a childlike question, "Mother, this is our stuff. Why are you giving this to somebody else? We would this way run short of the same."

Smiling and picking him in her lap, his mother said, "Son, always remember that charitable giving never reduces your possessions, rather this is a sign of prosperity. If a person is not in a position to give, he should still try to offer using his mind, words and deeds. Charity makes the person sincere towards his words and deeds and motivates him to work diligently."

Her words got ingrained in the mind of young Chanakya. He was quite brilliant in his student life from the very beginning. All his classmates used to receive knowledge as charity from him. Chanakya also would open heartedly offer them what they wanted. Apart from knowledge, he would offer all possible help to the needy. By the time he grew up, he had realised that her mother's words were so true. He had understood the magnificence of charity. Only the person who selflessly practises charitable giving as per his capacity gets rewarded.

Scientific Concept of Charity

By linking the idea of charity with its scientific concept, Chanakya had thousands of years ago proved that every action had an equal and opposite reaction. If a person instinctively helps somebody and readily offers charity, sooner or later he gets back the same many times multiplied. The tendency of accumulating for himself makes a person lonely whereas, the person who, despite having limited resources, is filled with the notion of charity is always successful in life. Chanakya used to say that living creatures are the main constituents of the Nature. Everybody is dependent on others. Hence, one should always nurture his instinct for charity. If people and the Nature stop charity, whatever they have accumulated would get destroyed. Even if trees do not give shelter to others or stop providing shade or fruits and flowers, they are destined to get destroyed only. Trees make their presence and importance felt by providing shade, fruits and flowers to people. In fact, charitable giving neither lowers a person not decreases his wealth. Instead, the person actually earns name and fame on account of that very charitable behaviour. However, the charity must be righteous. That should not involve vices like hypocrisy, dishonesty and greed. The charity loses its very significance if the same involves such vices. Chanakya made a lot of research to understand the notion of charity. He observed how and with how much struggle did the bees makehoney. Honey is very costly and healthy. Bees collectively make honey. When honey is ready, people using various means get hold of that honey. Even if bees do not give that honey, the same gets destroyed. The honey received from those bees is used by people in their medicines and meals. Honey has many beneficial properties. Bees are able to make their existence significant only because of the honey. Hence, the notion of charity should be kept alive even at the time of deprivation.

Chanakya used to say that living creatures are the main constituents of the Nature. Everybody is dependent on others. Hence, one should always nurture his instinct for charity. If people and the Nature stop charity, whatever they have accumulated would get destroyed. Even if trees do not give shelter to others or stop providing shade or fruits and flowers, they are destined to get destroyed only.

Chanakya, of course, devoted his entire life in the service of the country and in helping others. He believed that a self-centered life was hollow. A person should nurture for himself the goals that would help him serve his country. Chanakya was extremely brilliant. Had he so desired, he would have become a ruler himself. However, he believed that he could serve the country more by becoming a nation-builder. And he did the same. Chanakya won victory over many people with an amalgamation of his mind and intelligence. He induced many people to take the path of charity and gave proper direction to the lives of many others. He did not miss to give lessons even to common people from time to time.

A Person's Dignity

A person does not lose anything by giving, rather he actually gets back a lot. First of all, he gets a feeling of self-contentment. The notion of charity provides both physical and mental satisfaction. Chanakya would never miss to give a lesson on the magnificence of charity to a person who hesitated from giving. Once, Chanakya was passing by when he noticed a lady stopping her husband from making some charity. Her husband had pledged to make a donation for education of an orphan. When the lady came to know of the same, she said, "I have been asking you for so many days to get me new bangles but, every time you refuse claiming that you do not have enough money. If you did not have money, why did you at all take a vow to donate for an orphan's education?"

The husband replied, "Education is the right of a child. Hence, I do not consider jewellery more important than the donation for an orphan's education."

The lady sat down, feeling annoyed. Chanakya came to the husband and said, "Son, you are very sensible. You are very correct that giving donation for an orphan is the most righteous act. By doing this, you would not be deprived of anything, rather that help to an orphan would make you feel mentally satisfied."

The husband smiled and said with all modesty, "I will surely do that."

Chanakya then said to the lady, "Daughter, you are very lucky to have such a generous husband. Always remember that the beauty of your hand does not grow with bangles or jewellery. Instead, it would grow with charitable giving. When anybody donates to a needy person, the beauty of his hand shines with the jewellery of charity. I never advise giving to everybody or somebody undeserving but one should surely help a needy person."

Chanakya's words made that lady also understand the significance of charity.

Magnificence of Charity

Charity is just like a boomerang that returns to the giver many times multiplied. Once, a lady offered her glass full of milk to an stranger child suffering from thirst and hunger. Many years later, the same lady fell sick and fell over on a road. She was rushed to a hospital. The cost of her treatment there came to half a million rupees. When she came to her senses and learnt about the same, she was shocked.

Many a time, a charity that reaches a deserving person transforms the life of the receiver. In such a case, the magnificence of such a charity becomes ubiquitous. Charity is just like a boomerang that returns to the giver many times multiplied. Once, a lady offered her glass full of milk to an stranger child suffering from thirst and hunger. Many years later, the same lady fell sick and fell on a road. She was rushed to a hospital. The cost of her treatment there came to half a million rupees. When she came to her senses and learnt about the same, she was shocked. She did not have even a penny. When she went to the cash counter, she was told that the bill was already paid. The lady was asking about the person who made the payment when a young guy in a doctor's uniform came to her and said, "I have paid the bill, but believe me, this amount is still not enough to pay the price of the glass of milk that you had offered me when I was crying in pain out of thirst and hunger." The lady could not stop her tears.

Every person can donate as per his capacity and capability. Educating an illiterate, offering food to someone who is hungry, providing clothes to the needy and giving pencils and notebooks to poor children are all kinds of charitable giving only.

Donate to the Deserving, not to the Undeserving

Donation to an undeserving person is meaningless. Hence, Chanakya had, as part of his policy, made a recommendation for everybody to donate while staying away from donations to any undeserving person.

Chanakya believed that every person and creature should donate as per his or its capacity. That is the true dharma. God is one and He wants to see a man noble and righteous. When people tread the path of violence and immorality, it leads to anarchy in the society. This very anarchy spoils the entire environment. When people get hesitant to donate, others start scrambling for goods that become scarce. This results in destruction of goods and loss for people. Many a time, this even leads to loss of lives and property. On the other hand, if people start donating as per their capacity, this helps those living in deprivation. Everybody should practise charity, but charity should always be made to a deserving person only. Sometimes, a donation to an undeserving person results in various problems and difficulties. Donation to an undeserving person is meaningless. Hence, Chanakya had, as part of his policy, made a recommendation for everybody to donate while staying away from donations to any undeserving person.

No donations to the undeserving | **Donation Pot** | **Donate to the deserving**

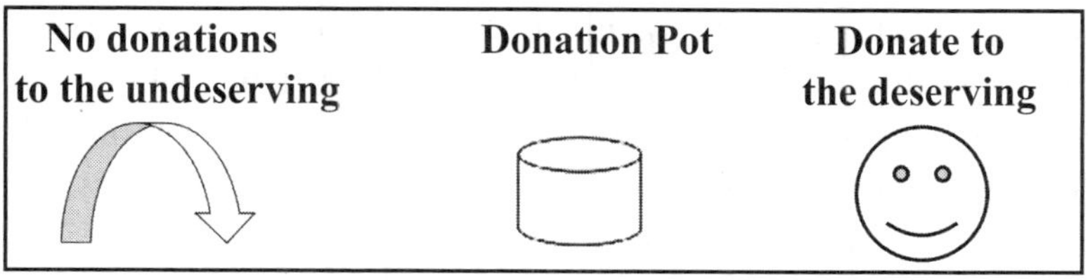

Lessons from Chanakya

Chanakya emphasises that everybody should practise charitable giving as per his capacity. Charity represents the prosperity of a person. If a person shows his willingness to donate even in a meagre state means, he is a true human being and deserves heaven. Prosperous people should surely practise charitable giving, as the existence of a human being is worthwhile only in helping other humans. That is the real humanity. Charity makes a man conscious of right and wrong and he himself follows a path of righteousness. A donation cannot be treated as a true charity if the same is given out of possessions accumulated through devious means. Only something given out of belongings earned with hard work and struggle is the best charity.

❑

Sports are Lessons of Life

Acharya's Pearls of Wisdom

- *Sports and life are interlinked.*
- *Those who play skilfully win the battle of their lives.*
- *There is not much of difference in planning for life and sport.*

Sports and Life

It has been millions of years since humans evolved on this earth. Charles Darwin has offered his thoughts on the evolution of humans in his book *Origin of Species*. It is believed that only apes can come close to the ancestors of humans. As time passed and as the humans evolved, their brain and personality also developed.

Neolithic Period or New Stone Age was a stage of development of human technology. Humans started using wild and domestic crops and domesticated animals during this period. The process of development went on like that for some time. Once the need for food was satisfied, humans started to look for avenues for entertainment. Entertainment gradually covered singing, music, dance and sports. Sports kept on evolving according to contemporary society and environment and people started enjoying the same. Today, besides cricket, football, volleyball, tennis, badminton, wrestling, boxing, etc., there are plenty of indoor games that may help a person get entertained during his leisure time. Not only that, modern gadgets have created, using the medium of mobiles, so many attractive games that may again come handy for anybody to enjoy whenever required. Sports and life are interlinked. Just as the life of a person is a playground, sports are the challenges of life. The person who is able to play these sports-like challenges adroitly is successful in the battle of life while the one who surrenders to those challenges out of fear or other reasons has to face failure. Chanakya was a very accomplished personality. He had linked sports to a person's life long ago. Not only that, he used his intelligence to develop a game that could help the players to easily understand the nitty-gritty of wars.

Kinds of Sports

Chanakya would always encourage the pupils in his gurukula to play games. When Chandragupta completed his studies, Chanakya one day said to him, "Chandragupta, even after you become a ruler, you would have to spare time for sports."

Chandragupta responded with surprise, "Guruji, how is that possible? A ruler would look very ridiculous as a player."

"Why would he look ridiculous? You should understand that sport is essential for every person. There are many ways to play sports - outdoors, indoors and others that can be played mentally. Sports may also be played in all fields of life. Schemes are played in mind with tact and prudence at every level, be it political, social or financial. However, people do not understand where and how to take a right step forward. These skills are attained by developing game strategy in mind. Hence, everybody should keep playing brain games in spare times."

Schemes are played in the mind with tact and prudence at every level, be it political, social or financial. However, people do not understand where and how to take a right step forward. These skills are attained by developing game strategy in mind. Hence, everybody should keep playing brain games in spare times.

Today, many new games have come up as brain games. Scrabble, crossword, quizzes, etc. are all examples of such brain games only. Every person should keep playing such games to sharpen his intelligence.

Hearing about the brain games, Chandragupta said, "Guruji, is there any game that can help in developing war strategies while staying within our palace? It's nice if it is already there, else there should be one."

"It's a very good suggestion. Very soon, you will have such a game that you would be able to play inside the palace and master the finer points of a battlefield," replied Chanakya.

Chaturang

Chandragupta was quite happy to hear that. He said, "Guruji, please let me know the rules of the game."

Chanakya arranged all the pieces of the game and said, "An army has mainly four kinds of forces - chariots, cavalry, elephants and infantry. Based on the four organs of army, this game has been given the name 'Chaturang'. Both the sides in the game shall start with equal number of chariots, cavalry, elephants and infantry."

Chanakya had a very sharp brain that could explore all kinds of fresh ideas. He decided to develop a game that could be played within a palace. He studied all the details and technicalities of a battlefield and designed a game using his intelligence. He went to Chandragupta and said, "I have developed a game for you. This is a war game. You would be able to play this game once you understand its specifics. As you go on attaining proficiency in this game, your brain also would go on getting sharper and developing strategic thinking skills. The game is to be played by two players and both would have equal rights."

Chandragupta was quite happy to hear that. He said, "Guruji, please let me know the rules of the game."

Chanakya arranged all the pieces of the game and said, "An army has mainly four kinds of forces - chariots, cavalry, elephants and infantry. Based on the four organs of army, this game has been given the name 'Chaturang'. Both the sides in the game shall start with equal number of chariots, cavalry, elephants and infantry."

"Guruji, if both the armies are equal in number, who will win the game and how?"

Chanakya smiled and replied, "You will know this only after playing. The player who puts into practice his strategic skills in a better way would win."

He then explained the rules of the game. Chanakya said, "You may play this game with any of your friends in your spare time and utilise the same for improving your ability to develop strategies and plans for battlefield."

This very game of 'Chaturang' is now known as 'Chess'. Many of the players in India viz. Vishwanathan Anand, Koneru Hampy, Tania Sachdev, Parimarjan Negi and Gukesh D have brought fame to India in this game on international level.

Smartness in Life

Why is it so that out of a lot of apparently similar looking persons, some are unhappy while the others are happy? One person is quite proficient in talking while the other does not have any idea of clarity. One person is quite active and intelligent while the other is passive and dull. This happens because some people do not plan their lives properly with smartness and intelligence and do not use their brain effectively. They accept the situation the way it exists. Just as a player has to make his plans to win the game, it is necessary to make plans in life also to lead the same successfully. Some people believe that it is burdensome and boring to lead this life with plans. They should then visualise playing their favourite games in their mind and ponder over the ways they would use to win the same. They should inculcate the same concept in their real lives i.e. they should be clear of their goals and make plans for the same.

To start with, prepare a chart on paper for all the activities right from the first day till the last day of the week. Though it may be hard initially but follow the activities as per chart for few days. By the time you complete 21 days following the chart scrupulously, you would have already made the set of activities in the chart part of your habit and thus you would have already taken your first step towards your goal.

If attaining the position of the highest officer in the country is your goal, you should make an outline of your plan for the same.

To start with, prepare a chart on paper for all the activities right from the first day till the last day of the week. Though it may be hard initially but follow the activities as per the chart for few days. By the time you complete 21 days following the chart scrupulously, you would have already made the set of activities in the chart part of your habit and thus you would have already taken your first step towards your goal.

Difference between a life plan and a game plan

There is not much of difference between a life plan and a game plan. Whereas a game requires a set of rules to be followed and practised in a disciplined manner, our life also involves creating a list of activities and abiding by the same. It's a game only in both the cases; just the playing fields are different. Whereas a regular game is played within a specified area, the playing field for a game of life is the entire life. It is never difficult for a person to attain success in life if the same is led skilfully in a disciplined way in accordance with plans. Though it appears that nobody would ever match Chanakya, it is not true. Even Chanakya himself maintained that a person brimming with virtue might reach the pinnacle of any field. Concentration, commitment and karma are the steps in the ladder of success. The stronger these steps are, the more confident a person will be to step on the same. If these steps start shaking, they would definitely make the person get unnerved. Hence, go ahead and make plans sincerely with concentration, commitment and karma and then march ahead on the path of your life. Have faith that, just like Chanakya, your brain, skills and intelligence also can conquer the strongest of forces.

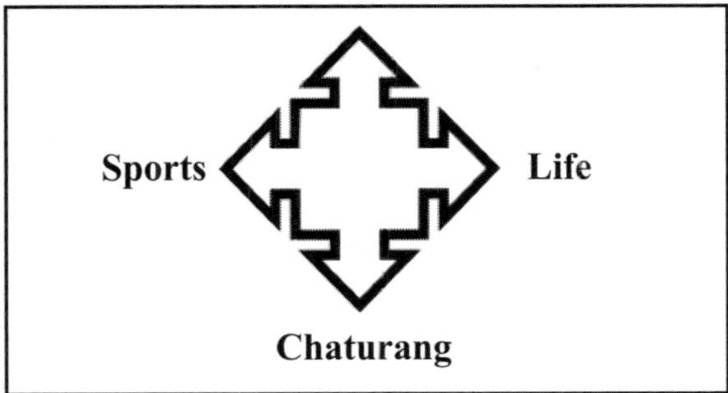

Lessons from Chanakya

Every person must spare some time out of his busy schedule for sports. It's not that sports may be enjoyed only during childhood. Life also is a playground and only the person who plays this game properly outperforms others.

Every person must spare some time for sports out of his busy schedule. It's not that sports may be enjoyed only during childhood. Life also is a playground and only the person who plays this game properly outperforms others. Different games and their rules make a person mature to progress in life and show him the path to overcome the obstacles. Besides physical games, mental and intellectual games are also very important and one should keep playing these games also. Such games enhance the mental ability of the person and improve his intelligence. While solving the puzzles of a game again and again, he learns the ways to solve the puzzles of life also.

❑

Measures to Get Over Problems

Acharya's Pearls of Wisdom

- *Health and wealth are two greatest assets of humans.*
- *Nobody can harm a person who is careful, wakeful and watchful.*
- *Grandness can be conquered by intelligence, ingenuity, energy and force.*
- *A man can cross all limits when faced with crisis.*
- *Cultured and prudent people face desperate circumstances courageously because of their ability to fight adverse situations.*

What are the problems?

People have discovered negativity in many positive words and have popularised them as such. Hence, even today, people often get frightened when they encounter a problem. This happens because, right from our childhood, a problem has been defined to us something as

'A job that is impossible to do,

'A situation that can paralyse a person' or

'A thing which, when encountered, can make a person lose his senses'.

Those who are afraid to face the problems never get to know those great opportunities concealed in them. Thousands of years ago, Chanakya had suggested ways that are still effective and shall remain effective for ages to come, for confronting as well as solving problems. These solutions and strategies prove to be decisive in making our lives better.

The above comments are made in reference to problems. Thus, it gets ingrained in the minds of people right in their childhood itself that problems are obstructive. On the other hand, the reality is that existence of problems is a good sign in the life of a person. Problems make the person realise that he is alive. How could there be any existence of problems when there is no life? In fact, the problems are another form of challenges. Just a change in its name changes the perception in people's mind. Whereas the problems appear to be painful, challenges make the progress in life profound. Problems and challenges are different manifestations hidden under the same veil and once the veil is removed, they become visible distinctly. Hence, try to firmly ingrain this fact in your subconscious mind that problems are nothing but challenges - the challenges that are essential for ceaselessly moving ahead on the path to your goal. Existence of problems is not a matter to be concerned about, rather absence of problems is definitely a matter of worry. Great opportunities often come shrouded by problems. Those who are afraid to face the problems never get to know those great opportunities concealed in them. Thousands of years ago, Chanakya had suggested ways that are still effective and shall remain effective for ages to come, for confronting as well as solving problems. These solutions and strategies prove to be decisive in making our lives better.

Saam, Daam, Dand, Bhed

A person once asked Acharya Chanakya, "Acharya, everybody cherishes desire to be successful but why is it so that only a few people are able to attain success?"

Chanakya explained, "This happens as people do not have the habit of building strategies before taking action. Hence, they give in to the problems confronting them, assuming them to be mountainous and thus they themselves invite defeat."

The person said, "OK, that means a problem should be solved by discussions and mutual understanding."

"Yes." Chanakya continued after thinking for a moment, "Many a time, some people are filled with greed and self-interest and they always look for their personal benefits. If the resolution to a problem requires managing such a person, he should be removed out of the way by paying a Daam."

"I didn't follow. Which are those strategies that may be tried when faced with problems? Kindly let me know in detail."

"I believe that the strategies of 'Saam, Daam, Dand and Bhed' should be used to get over the problems. For a person who intelligently uses them, the problems always come to them in the form of opportunities."

The person requested, "Acharya, could you please explain clearly the types of strategies and how they should be tried out?"

"I am just telling that there are four ways to tackle a problem. All these four methods should be used according to the circumstances and opportunities. Many a time, the problem is so simple that everything gets resolved just by mutual discussion.

There is no need for any attack in such a case. A prudent person understands everything by logic. This is called Saam."

The person said, "OK, that means a problem should be resolved by discussions and mutual understanding."

"Yes." Chanakya continued after thinking for a moment, "Many a time, some people are filled with greed and self-interest and they always look for their personal benefits. If the resolution to a problem requires managing such a person, he should be removed out of the way by paying a Daam."

"How should a problem be tackled when that person does not succumb to Saam and Daam?"

"In that case, the policy of 'divide and rule' should be applied and internal conflicts should be created among opponents. This only is known as Bhed."

"What should be done when the strategies of Saam, Daam and Bhed also fail?"

"In that case, only one strategy is left - Dand. The enemy must be inflicted a severe punishment in such a situation. The form of punishment may depend on the time and circumstances."

"Acharya, if even the strategy of Dand is not appropriate for a situation, what should be done?"

Acharya, being little enraged, replied, "The strategies of Saam, Daam, Dand and Bhed are capable of securing victory over any problem. Even these strategies should be used only if so required and when the same is meant for common good. For personal problems, one should keep his head cool. A cool head and patience, in a very short time, proves this to be true that personal problems are most of the time baits for great opportunities. Had I not treated the problems in my childhood as opportunities, I would have never been at a position where I am today."

The person was by now completely in agreement with Acharya's point of view that a sharp intelligence could surmount any problem.

How do Saam, Daam, Dand and Bhed only solve problems?

When the problems are the result of wrong decisions, the person should accept that he himself is part of the problem and its solution also has to pass through him. Facing the problem responsibly and finding a solution with intelligence is what is known as Saam. Every problem may be transformed into an opportunity with deftness and prudence. Hence, you should not panic when faced with a problem, instead confront the same courageously with patience.

Saam: Any person may experience setbacks and lose his balance any time in his life. Even if we assume that such setbacks are in the hands of destiny, getting back to life after the same is entirely in the hands of that person. A human is never endowed with all the good qualities. He does have some or other shortcomings and they are there as very existence of the shortcomings makes the human complete. If these shortcomings were not there, the humans would step into the league of gods and where there is God, the existence of humans would start disappearing. For this human life to go on, it's essential for the mistakes, shortcomings and problems to be there, rather they must be there. Many a time, people are not able to control some of the problems in their lives, but most of the problems are also created by wrong choices and incorrect decisions made by them. When the problems are the result of wrong decisions, the person should accept that he himself is part of the problem and its solution also has to pass through him. Facing the problem responsibly and finding a solution with intelligence is what is known as Saam. Every problem may be transformed into an opportunity with deftness and prudence. Hence, you should not panic when faced with a problem, instead confront the same courageously with patience.

Daam: Chanakya believes wealth is a true friend at the time of a disaster. Hence, one should accumulate wealth so that the same could be used for resolving problems when faced with a disaster. Many a time, the paucity of wealth only forces a person to remain isolated. Hence, people should earn wealth from a good and legitimate means only. They should spend for themselves and their families prudently following some budget plans so that they always have enough to pay the Daam to resolve a problem when required. Many times, quite a few problems arise on account of health and family issues. Daam is needed more for resolving problems arising from sickness and disaster. Chanakya presents a different perspective in this regard also. He mentions that, many a time, a person with greedy tendency even divulges enemy's confidential information when tempted with Daam. If Daam is required to be paid for obtaining such information in the interest of the country, such a payment should certainly be made, as just paying a Daam would resolve a big problem and especially the country could be kept secured.

Bhed: These days, people often believe more in personal happiness and hence they don't even miss any opportunity to create conflicts among others when faced with a problem. Chanakya considers the policy of 'Divide and Rule' a strategy under 'Bhed'. However, he recommends its usage only when the same is required for common good and for the benefit of the country. Chanakya never advises to harm somebody for personal benefit. He always had the interest of the country in his mind. It was for building a great country only that he dedicated his entire life in the interest of the country.

Chanakya considers the policy of 'Divide and Rule' a strategy under 'Bhed'. However, he recommends its usage only when the same is required for common good and for the benefit of the country. Chanakya never advises to harm somebody for personal benefit. He always had the interest of the country in his mind.

Dand: Dand is necessary as, in its absence, the 'fish law' starts taking root, meaning big fish start eating small fish. Such a situation is immoral and improper for any country and that's why Chanakya has emphasised usage of Dand. Many a time, a criminal, despite being warned, does not stop committing heinous crimes. Punishing him with a Dand, that also a severe one, becomes sensible in such a case. Dand helps in evading misfortunes and problems and establishing security and welfare.

End of Problems

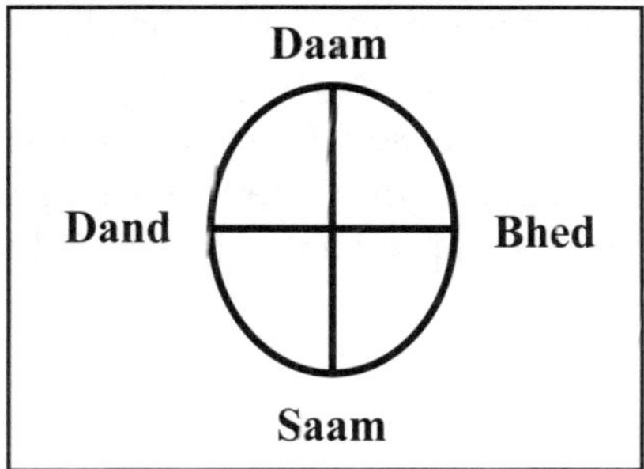

Problem Resolution

Chanakya exhorts people to unhesitatingly face the problems instead of trying to evade them. If somebody manages to somehow evade the problems, they come back to face him in an extremely monstrous form. Hence, when faced with problems, try to resolve them as soon as possible. The problems in such a case take the form of opportunities and offer benefits only to the person. One should take responsibility for all his actions. People who, instead of taking responsibility for their mistakes, try to pass on the buck to others have to ultimately struggle with those problems themselves only. A person may easily resolve many of his problems just by courageously accepting his mistakes and assuming responsibilities.

Lessons from Chanakya

Chanakya suggests that problems should be resolved tactfully. One should use the strategy of Saam, Daam, Dand and Bhed for the same. People who use right strategy for resolving problems are successful. One should never panic when faced with problems.

Chanakya suggests that problems should be resolved tactfully. One should use the strategy of Saam, Daam, Dand and Bhed for the same. People who use right strategy for resolving problems are successful. One should never panic when faced with problems. They should be dealt with courageously and unhesitatingly. Don't try to evade problems. Those who evade problems have to face them in more monstrous form at a time when they are completely exhausted and busy finding suitable place for taking rest.

❑

Power of Music

Acharya's Pearls of Wisdom

- *Among mantras, the Gayatri Mantra is the most powerful and fulfiller of all desires.*
- *Music, besides providing relaxation, fills a person with concentration, enthusiasm and self-confidence.*
- *Sound of music makes even a difficult path effortless.*
- *Music provides infinite dimensions of life to a person.*

Music

What is music? It's a composition that is created with a combination of instruments, dance and melody. Music is an art for expression of emotions with the help of notes and melody. Music has been accorded significance in Indian Vedas also. 'Samaveda' is a collection of those Vedic verses that are singable. Ever since ancient times, puja and prayers are being performed by way of singing. Fine arts refer to these five arts - music, poetry, painting, sculpture and architecture. Out of these five arts, music has been given the highest status as the sound of music leads people from the state of hopelessness to that of hope. Musical notes and sound waves emanating from them shake the chords inside a person's mind. Crystal clear sounds of music prepare a person not only to recoup everything that he has lost but also to venture out for new achievements. Dr A. P. J. Kalam, a great scientist the former President of our country, considered music to be the best means for relaxation. He had said, "I feel relaxed after a music practice. When I feel tired, I just pick up my Veena and get lost in the musical sounds of its strings. Musical tones of Veena eliminate my entire physical and mental tiredness. For me, playing Veena is just a mental relaxation, a music sadhana, a Bhav Samadhi."

Legends of Music

Seven notes of music are parts of ॐ only. The word ॐ is the origin of music notes and words. This word is considered as the entire world for music. Chanakya not only was aware of the power of music but he himself was a great admirer of music also.

Music has been accorded great significance in India right from the mythological times. We have read in mythological scriptures that even God felt infinite peace in music melodies. The goddess of knowledge Maa Saraswati had imparted the knowledge of music to Narada. Whenever Narada visited any place playing his Veena and chanting 'Narayan-Narayan', he would not return from there without securing a solution to his problem. It is believed that Narada passed on this knowledge of music to Bharat Muni who in turn, through his Natya Shastra, popularised and propagated music among common people.

Origin of Music

Indian music is believed to have originated from Vedas. The word ॐ (Om) is made primarily of three phonetic syllables - a, u and m. All three letters together make the word ॐ. It is believed that these three letters represent the creative powers of Brahma, Vishnu and Mahesh respectively - Brahma the creator, Vishnu the preserver and Mahesh the destroyer of the Universe. The three letters have been picked up from Indian Vedas - the Rigveda, the Samaveda and the Yajurveda. Seven notes of music are parts of ॐ only. The word ॐ is the origin of music notes and words. This word is considered as the entire world for music. Chanakya not only was aware of the power of music but he himself was a great admirer of music also. Hence, whenever Chandragupta felt exhausted after attending to his various engagements and state affairs, Chanakya would immediately arrange for melodious music for him. Music would help Chandragupta come out of the interruptions of state affairs and get filled with fresh energy and enthusiasm.

Chanakya was Aware of the Power of Music

Chandragupta once asked Chanakya, "Acharya, you often make me enjoy music. Could you please let me know what after all special power this music has that makes you believe the same to be so essential for a king as well as for the soldiers?"

Chanakya smiled and replied, "Our Vedas contain detailed information relating to music. As per Vedas, the sound of Om is the origin of the universe. It is a Pranav mantra. Music is considered to be a gift from divine powers. When this is divided into seven swaras (notes), they are called 'Sapta Sur' or 'Sargam'. These seven swaras only create music."

Chandragupta interrupted, "Those seven swaras are 'Sa Re Ga Ma Pa Dha and Ni'".

It's very necessary to have a strong mind to use the brain effectively. This mind is quite flickering. It keeps creating chaos in a person's heart and music is the best means to keep it under control. Music not only develops positive thinking of a person but also keeps him temperate. Besides providing relaxation, music also fills a person with concentration, self-confidence and enthusiasm.

"Correct! These seven swaras are made enjoyable with the help of melody and lyrics. Just as the beauty of a girl gets boosted by jewelleries, musical sounds become more pleasing with melodies and lyrics. These musical sounds have the capacity to vibrate the nerves of every person."

Chandragupta was listening to Chanakya very attentively. He said, "Acharya, why should music be necessary in politics?"

"Because politics is a brain game. It's very necessary to have a strong mind to use the brain effectively. This mind is quite flickering. It keeps creating chaos in a person's heart and music is the best means to keep it under control. Music not only develops positive thinking of a person but also keeps him temperate. Besides providing relaxation, music also fills a person with concentration, self-confidence and enthusiasm."

"Now only I understand why I used to often wake up to melodious sounds of music. This was also a part of your strategy only."

"Certainly! A musical melody transmitting positive energy helps in keeping a person fresh for the whole day. A prayer is also a form of music only. Not only that, the chirping of birds, ringing of bells, burbling of waterfalls and babbling of rivers, they all have music. They all provide calmness to our hearts and eyes. Many a time, a person goes on to even discover innovative ideas while listening to relaxing music. Music is able to even define the personality of a person."

"How is that?" asked Chandragupta with surprise.

Looking at the enquiring eyes of Chandragupta, Chanakya smiled and said, "It's like this. If a person is fond of listening fast music, he is extrovert i.e. talkative by nature and if anybody generally listens to soft and slow music, he is intelligent and sensitive. Music takes a person towards divinity."

Chanakya affirms, "The radiance of knowledge helps in getting rid of worldly fears." Thus, there is no doubt that the power of music is limitless and mystifying. Captivating music reforms the life of a person and even helps him reach the pinnacle of success.

After listening to the words of Chanakya, Chandragupta also was now well aware of the power of music.

Musical Instruments and Their Varieties

There are many forms of music but two of them are quite popular - classical music and folk music. Many new forms of music have become popular in this modern age, but the impact that classical and folk music have and the sweetness they possess are unique. Classical music is based on scriptures and folk music keeps on developing based on period and place. Melodies of music are played on instruments like sitar, tabla, dholak, flute, sarod, violin, veena, shehnai, santoor and mridangam. Musical tunes emanating from these instruments transform the distress of a person into his enthusiasm. And then, even a dreadful path becomes quite effortless for that person. Music uncovers the knowledge of a person. Chanakya affirms, "The radiance of knowledge helps in getting rid of worldly fears." Thus, there is no doubt that the power of music is limitless and mystifying. Captivating music reforms the life of a person and even helps him reach the pinnacle of success. The entire world knows about Tansen, one of the Navaratnas in the court of Emperor Akbar. A common adage is quite popular in his town Gwalior even today that children there cry in musical tunes and stones roll over in rhythm. The musical rendition by Tansen had the power to the extent that Deepak Raga sung by him could generate flames of fire and Megha Raga could douse the same.

Chanakya hence considers the power of music to be significant in the life of a person. Music provides unlimited dimensions of life to a person.

Music is Everywhere

Chanakya has not considered music so powerful for nothing. Music is everywhere. Music is in life as well as in death. Music is in cries. Music is in humour. Music is in the Nature and in the entire living world. Even a war cry has the rhythm and tune of music. Music is played at the time of war; even civilian instrumentalists are part of an army. Indian armed forces like Sikh Regiment, Gorkha Brigade, Army Service Corps, Rajputana Rifles and Madras Regiment still have the custom of formal war cries. Sikh Regiment has 'Jo Bole So Nihal, Sat Sri Akal' as its war cry whereas Gorkha Brigade's war cry is 'Jai Ma Kali, Aayo Gorkhali'. Similarly, the war cry for Madras Regiment is 'Veera Madrassi, Adi Kollu, Adi Kollu, Adi Kollu'. When the band contingent of the army, playing a melodious patriotic tune, passes by the onlookers, a sense of patriotism gets developed in them.

Chanakya hence considers the power of music to be significant in the life of a person. Music provides unlimited dimensions of life to a person.

Music

Vedas	**Musical Instruments**	**Instruments**	**The Nature**	**Om**	**War**
⇨	⇨	⇨	⇨	⇨	⇨

Lessons from Chanakya

It's essential for a statesman to keep listening to serene music on regular basis. While attending to various state affairs, the mind has to remain active and engaged in multiple tasks. This results in physical as well as mental exhaustion. Music generates agility in both mind and body and fills a person with fresh energy. This is the reason that melodies of music exist in war as well as in all the parts of the Nature. While these melodies exist somewhere in the form of birds, springs, rivers, streams, leaves and trees, the same emanate at other places from musical instruments like flute and veena to mesmerise everybody. Chanakya's words spoken ages ago are meaningful even today. Listening to a melodious music not only provides relaxation when a person is worried or distressed but also opens a number of options for resolving problems.

❑

Ruler versus Leader

Acharya's Pearls of Wisdom

- *'I have in any case got control of the kingdom' - this thinking should not result in iniquitous treatment being meted out to the people. The rule of such a tyrannical ruler perishes just as the youth and beauty (Succumb to old age).*
- *A ruler who is competent and people's saviour, is adored, irrespective of the size of his kingdom, by the entire world and is always successful in all his endeavours.*
- *A ruler who adjudicates based on the four principles of truth, evidence, witness and law conquers the entire world.*

History is a witness to the fact that whenever persons with strong ideological backgrounds gained control of thrones, their countries along with the lives of common people have undergone significant progress. President Ronald Reagan is even today revered by the people not only in the United States of America but the entire world. He was a hero and a leader in true sense. His leadership qualities had taken him to the pinnacle of success.

Who is a Ruler?

Only a person who is blessed with human values and who has honesty, self-confidence, courage and leadership qualities may prove to be a worthy ruler. A ruler and a leader are two sides of the same coin. Chanakya considers only that person worthy of a ruler who can take care of his subjects with morality and humility. Chanakya was an extraordinarily learned man. His sharp mind was aware that a ruler should be educated, cultured and courageous. He considered education essential for a ruler. He believed in the dictum 'Just as a mad elephant destroys everything, an uneducated ruler destroys his kingdom'. A ruler and a leader are the same. Only a ruler who always gives priority to the interest of his subjects is actually worthy of being called a ruler. Chanakya had made a lot of efforts to make Chandragupta Maurya a good emperor and he had effectively brought out those of his qualities that were essential for a competent ruler. Chanakya had authored the treatise Arthashastra with his pen name Kautilya. This is a massive work spread in15 volumes and 160 chapters. The subjects treated in detail in this work include duties of a ruler, appointment of ministers, appointment of secret agents, periodic appraisals and supervision of armed forces, forts and palaces as well as strategies for protection from enemies. Chanakya has mentioned in the first five verses of the 19th chapter in the first volume of Arthashastra - 'If a ruler is energetic, his subjects would also be equally energetic. If he is careless, lethargic and sluggish in his works, his subjects also would be lethargic and they would empty his coffers. Not only that, a careless ruler can easily get into the claws of enemy. Hence, a ruler himself should always remain energetic and active.' History is witness to the fact that whenever persons with strong ideological backgrounds gained control of thrones, their countries along with the lives of common people have undergone significant progress. President Ronald Reagan is even today revered by the people not only in the United States of America but the entire world. He was a hero and a leader in true sense. His leadership qualities had taken him to the pinnacle of success.

Ronald Reagan, A True Leader

One day, an important meeting of President Ronal Reagan and the members of his cabinet was in progress. A discussion on a policy framed by General Collin Powell and members of the cabinet was going on in that meeting. Ronald Reagan did not like the strategy proposed by Powell and other members, but considering the favourable opinions of all other people in the meeting, he accorded his approval to take the proposal forward. Reagan used to have confidence in everybody. The policy was implemented and within a very short time, the policy was declared to be unsuccessful. There was widespread dismay - why did President Reagan implement such an ineffective policy? Media tried to corner him. All the media people were anxious to get all details of this failed policy from him. One journalist asked him, "Sir, was this policy framed by you or somebody else is responsible for this mess?"

President Reagan responded calmly, "Of course this was entirely my idea. However, I would like to tell you a fact about myself. I can make a mistake once but would never repeat the same."

Keeping his subjects and ministers well protected in every situation is the most important merit of a good ruler. Such a ruler is revered not only during his lifetime but remains immortal even after his death.

In modern times, a leader only is known as a ruler. Only the leader who keeps the interest of common people supreme can lead the country towards progress.

With this statement, he saved reputation of General Powell and all the members of his cabinet, else they all would have had to face public anger. General Powell was also present there at that time. He was in tears the moment he heard President Reagan owning all the responsibility. He realised that President Reagan was having the feeling of concern. He was conscious of the situation in which Powell and all the members of the cabinet were there at that time. It was only by placing himself in their situation that the President not only preserved their reputation but also prevented their mistake from coming to light in front of the public. At that very moment, General Powell made the decision to serve President Reagan for his entire life. His this very quality of respecting others and having faith in them made President Reagan immortal.

Thus, President Reagan saved the cabinet ministers by owning full responsibility for their mistakes. They all remained indebted to President Reagan for their entire lives. All the assertions made in the Arthashastra of Chanakya were proven right in the above incident. Keeping his subjects and ministers well protected in every situation is the most important merit of a good ruler. Such a ruler is revered not only during his lifetime but remains immortal even after his death.

In modern times, a leader only is known as a ruler. Only the leader who keeps the interest of common people supreme can lead the country towards progress.

Qualities of a Ruler According to Chanakya

As per Chanakya, 'A ruler always has internal and external threats.' Hence, it is necessary for him to possess many qualities.

The most important quality out of them is that the ruler must be perseverant, knowledgeable and educated.

Man is mortal. He has to meet his end someday. Hence, the ruler should keep an eye on persons who, in addition to being competent leaders, are benevolent, courageous and honest. A man's deeds only make him a king. Hence, he always kept reasonable watch on the deeds of Chandragupta and corrected him wherever possible.

Education perfects a person and provides maturity to his mind and intelligence. Chanakya has clearly defined the qualities and duties of a ruler. Chanakya was a very able and intelligent teacher. Right from his childhood, he had trodden a path full of thorns and had gone through all kinds of pains and struggles. He always cherished the dream of building such an India where a ruler conducted himself as a father to his subjects for their welfare and well-being. He believed that a ruler was expected to possess all the greatest qualities as subjects always followed the example of their ruler. A ruler must have full knowledge of the condition of his state including financial gains, loss, treasury, people and armed forces. He should, on his own, periodically ascertain the well-being of his subjects. He should visit and personally offer respect to the gifted scholars in his kingdom and honour them suitably. Man is mortal. He has to meet his end someday. Hence, the ruler should keep an eye on persons who, in addition to being competent leaders, are benevolent, courageous and honest. A man's deeds only make him a king. Hence, he always kept reasonable watch on the deeds of Chandragupta and corrected him wherever possible.

The First and The Last Goal of a Ruler

Chanakya always guided Chandragupta to the right path. Chandragupta went on to become a great emperor only because of the principles and policies he learnt from Chanakya. One day, Chanakya asked Chandragupta, "Now you are discharging your duties as a ruler towards your people. Are you aware what should be the first and the last goal of a ruler?"

Finding Chandragupta lost in thoughts, Chanakya continued, "The first and the last goal of a ruler should be the happiness of his subjects. Do you know when the subjects are happy?"

"Acharya, when the interests of the subjects are fulfilled, they get happy," replied Chandragupta.

"Not only that, besides their interests, the ruler should keep a close eye on the happenings in his state. Punishing the culprits suitably when required is also a major function of a leadership. Yes, the ruler, when awarding a punishment, should keep in mind that justice has to be equal for all. A criminal is just a criminal for the ruler even if he is related to him." Chanakya said.

"Chandragupta, you should also make sure that, though you are competent to take all decisions, experienced and brilliant ministers and gurus are always consulted. Many a time, a ruler gets overburdened with so many problems and works that he is not able to take appropriate decisions. Hence, never forget your gurus and dependable ministers."

Chandragupta was listening to Chanakya very attentively. He said, "I will always ensure that all convicts are treated uniformly and awarded punishments after due consideration."

"Chandragupta, you should also make sure that, though you are competent to take all decisions, experienced and brilliant ministers and gurus are always consulted. Many a time, a ruler gets overburdened with so many problems and works that he is not able to take appropriate decisions. Hence, never forget your gurus and dependable ministers."

"Yes Acharya! I will always keep this in mind and also my first and the last goal while discharging my responsibilities."

Chanakya felt happy and said, "India is now in safe hands."

A Ruler should Exercise Care as Following:

Should keep his plans secret: A ruler should first execute all his plans. He should not make them public before implementation.

Deadlines for projects should be set: Many a time, a project is initiated without setting any definite timelines for the same. In such a case, the project usually gets held up and remains unfinished. Hence, a ruler should get all his ventures completed within definite timelines in a planned way.

Periodic review: Chanakya says that as human mind is unstable, a ruler or leader should periodically review the works executed by his subordinates.

Allocation of Duties for Personnel and Subordinates: A ruler should make clear allocation of the jobs to the people working for him so that they may attend to the same honestly without difficulty. Not only that, the ruler should cleverly keep reading even the minds of his subordinates. This way only he would be able to make sure that his subordinates stay honest and not involved in corruption.

Ruler versus Leader

Objectives

Caution

Quality

Being Vigilant: A ruler should be absolutely vigilant both on internal and external fronts. Chanakya says that the ruler should keep a watchful eye on all areas. A disaster may be waiting to strike the moment you waver your concentration.

Happiness of a ruler lies in the happiness of his subjects. Welfare of the subjects is the biggest benevolence for a ruler. It is the duty of a ruler to accord priority to the well-being of his subjects over his own happiness. Being a ruler does not mean getting immersed in self-gratification, rather he should follow the path of simplicity and righteousness. The ruler who enjoys luxury and self-gratification and has tendency to be angry and greedy meets his end very soon.

Lessons from Chanakya

Happiness of a ruler lies in the happiness of his subjects. Welfare of the subjects is the biggest benevolence for a ruler. It is the duty of a ruler to accord priority to the well-being of his subjects over his own happiness. Being a ruler does not mean getting immersed in self-gratification, rather he should follow the path of simplicity and righteousness. The ruler who enjoys luxury and self-gratification and has tendency to be angry and greedy meets his end very soon. A ruler should have control over his senses and should march ahead on his path of karma and lead his state and subjects towards growth and development. That only is the true karma for a ruler.

❑

Power of Solitude

Acharya's Pearls of Wisdom

- *Only one person resolves to march ahead; all the rest just follow him.*
- *Despite being surrounded by many relatives, friends, wife, children, etc., man is absolutely alone in this world.*

Solitude

The maxim that 'a gram can't bust the oven alone' has been popular for ages. The maxim may be partially true but this is entirely incorrect to say that a single person can't do anything. In fact, it may be observed that an individual only creates history, attains spectacular success and leaves behind a trail of such inspirational imprints that always make the coming generations understand that an individual person is generally the most courageous. Chanakya also agreed to this notion completely. Once, some of his pupils asked him, "How can a single person bring about a change or alter the circumstances?" And Chanakya had then clarified, "A single person only makes a new beginning and marches ahead towards his goal. Others just follow him."

One of the pupils remarked, "It's a difficult job to take responsibility for a big task all alone."

And then Acharya had responded, "It's certainly difficult but definitely not impossible."

Chanakya was a very honest, intelligent and learned person and he did not like to indulge in obsequiousness towards Dhanananda. He was outspoken. He had the courage to tell the truth forthrightly. Dhanananda did not like him at all because of these very reasons. One day, he insulted Chanakya and got him thrown out of his court. Chanakya was alone in that difficult situation. Some people did have sympathy with him but they had no courage to stand by him.

Acharya would often tell his pupils, "Difficulty is just like the devil that keeps many precious gifts and unlimited success in his possession. However, it's necessary to bring that devil under command in order to get hold of those gifts and success."

The individuals who have the courage to take initiatives and are bursting with self-confidence may change history with their constant endeavours and struggles and bring a new dawn for everybody.

Power of Single Chanakya

Chanakya had mastered the Vedas and started to understand the specifics of politics in a very short time. He had obtained practical and experimental knowledge at Taxila. He then continued there as a teacher and taught many students. The tyrannical, immoral and ruthless ruler of Pataliputra King Dhanananda insulted Chanakya.

Chanakya was a very honest, intelligent and learned person and he did not like to indulge in obsequiousness towards Dhanananda. He was outspoken. He had the courage to tell the truth forthrightly. Dhanananda did not like him at all because of these very reasons. One day, he insulted Chanakya and got him thrown out of his court. Chanakya was alone in that difficult situation. Some people did have sympathy with him but they had no courage to stand by him. After being thrown out by the tyrant ruler, Chanakya did not waver despite losing the means for livelihood and despite having no support from others; instead, he remained steady with persistence and kept making efforts to regain and strengthen his position.

A common man may take any destructive step after getting shaken badly. However, Chanakya bravely confronted his adverse circumstances. It was only based on his experience in facing problems that he wrote in his Chanakya Niti, "If a person gets surrounded by problems, difficulties and adversities, he should brave them with fearlessness, courage and patience. They can be surmounted only this way." It was only after that insult by Dhanananda that he vowed not to sit quiet until he had Dhanananda over-thrown completely. This vow of Chanakya obliterated all his problems, else it was certainly not simple and easy to take such a difficult vow even in the absence of comforts, means and resources.

Chanakya attained all this just alone. Many people joined him gradually, but the initiative was always taken by Chanakya. In other words, Chanakya was the lone traveller on his path and other people were just following him and marking the trail left behind by him.

Chanakya, on the strength of his intelligence, shrewdness and knowledge, not only defeated Alexander but also dislodged Dhanananda completely. He installed an able person like Chandragupta as emperor of India. The process of making Chandragupta an emperor got completed in the supervision of

Chanakya only. When the name and fame of Chandragupta started spreading all around, Chanakya also started receiving acclaim for the same.

Chanakya attained all this just alone. Many people joined him gradually, but the initiative was always taken by Chanakya. In other words, Chanakya was the lone traveller on his path and other people were just following him and marking the trail left behind by him.

In Modern Times also, A Single Person Only is Strong

Chanakya had said ages ago that a person had to complete all his jobs alone only. A person, despite having a family, is alone as he departs this life alone only. He is born also alone. Man also has to reap the outcome of his deeds alone only. He becomes a part of golden history only after treading this worldly path all alone.

Otherwise also, a person may not be able to move on for long taking help from the others. One cannot reach the summit with the help of crutches. A person may be able to walk slowly with assistance from others whereas he may reach the sky on the strength of his own feet. If you walk with assistance from others, you will have to stop where others stop. On the other hand, you are master of your own will when you are all alone. And if you have a sense of enthusiasm, self-confidence and responsibility, you may perhaps never have to stop at all. You will soon reach your destination.

This amazing feat of Colin has proved that a single person, assimilating his hopes and confidence at double the speed, can make an impossible task possible and can make even a barren land fertile.

The person who possesses wings of hope, honesty, enthusiasm, courage and confidence has the capacity to even cross oceans all alone. When a person marches ahead alone, he transforms even impossible challenges into achievable ones. He amazes the world with such extraordinary achievements that had been thus far dumped by history into a list of improbabilities declared to be unachievable by humans.

Colin O'Brady of the United States of America has become the first person to cross Antarctica all alone without any kind of assistance. It took 54 days for around 33-years old Colin to cover the distance of 1600 km across ice-covered continent. Before him, Borge Ousland of Norway was the first person to complete solo crossing of Antarctica but he had used kite assistance for determining wind direction. This amazing feat of Colin has proved that a single person, assimilating his hopes and confidence at double the speed, can make an impossible task possible and can make even a barren land fertile.

Medical facilities currently available around the world have been built based on the discoveries of individuals only. Many fearless individuals have attained success with concentration with the help of their courage and hard work. Chanakya used to say that when an individual focused his concentration in the right direction, no obstacle in this world would be able to stop him.

Padma Shri awardee Jamuna Tudu is a social worker. After marriage, she shifted from her small native village in Odisha to Jharkhand. She felt extremely happy to see the greenery at her new place. But her happiness did not last long. She came to know very soon that forest mafia was blatantly yelling precious trees in the forest without any permission and making heavy profit by selling them. She started feeling quite distressed to find the trees disappearing gradually. Finally, one day she made up her mind, took four more women volunteers with her and left for the forest armed with heavy clubs in their hands. The women were able to chase away all the mafia men with the help of their clubs. Mafia people did attack these women. However, seeing the courage of the women, especially Jamuna Tudu, even the men from her village came out to stand by her. This resulted in reduction in incidents of tree-felling and gradually, the stories of courage and bravery of Jamuna Tudu started spreading all around. The widespread sparkle of her acts of valour finally got her the award of Padma Shri from the Government of India in January 2019.

This notion has been prevalent since ages that women are weaker as compared to men. But, women like Jamuna Tudu have debased this archaic notion and signified the belief of Chanakya that even a single person only plays a decisive role in changing history.

Recognise the Power of Solitude

Man is a social animal. Hence, he cannot live alone. This is true, but at the same time, this also is true that if a person wants to attain something great and invent something new in his life, he would have to march ahead alone only. The crowd often keeps following the things and practices that have been prevalent since ages and many a time, a person has to fight against not only his society or country but also the entire world for bringing about something new and original meant for common good. History is replete of examples where people with trailblazing ideas had to face innumerable obstacles but they just didn't care about them. Medical facilities currently available around the world have been built based on the discoveries of individuals only. Many fearless individuals have attained success on the strength of their focus, courage and hard work. Chanakya used to say that when an individual focused his attention in the right direction, no obstacle in this world would be able to stop him.

A Gram Can't Break the Oven

The maxim 'a single gram can't break the oven' has been popular for ages. Maxims also should change with time. These maxims were created at a time when man was not aware of his strengths and limits. In ancient times, man used to wander looking for food only. When these necessities started getting fulfilled comfortably, he started exploring knowledge. For ages, women have been considered to be weak, but even women have proved single-handedly that one has to fight this world alone only and refine himself like gold to attain excellence.

Who can say after watching the stunts of Captain Surabhi of Daredevils Team of the Indian Army that 'a single gram can't break the oven'? What to talk of the oven, a single person can even move mountains with his courage, bravery and determination.

Today, women have earned name and fame in every walk of life. Even in the army, women have been touching the sky with their fearlessness and courage. Somewhere Lieutenant Bhavana Kasturi is leading 144 men contingent of the Army Service Corps while somewhere else, Captain Bhavna Syal of the armed forces is leading her contingent. At the same time, a woman like Lieutenant Ambika Sudhakaran is leading a contingent of Navy at some other place. Who can say after watching the stunts of Captain Surabhi of Daredevils Team of the Indian Army that 'a single gram can't break the oven'? What to talk of the oven, a single person can even move mountains with his courage, bravery and determination.

The Line of Success

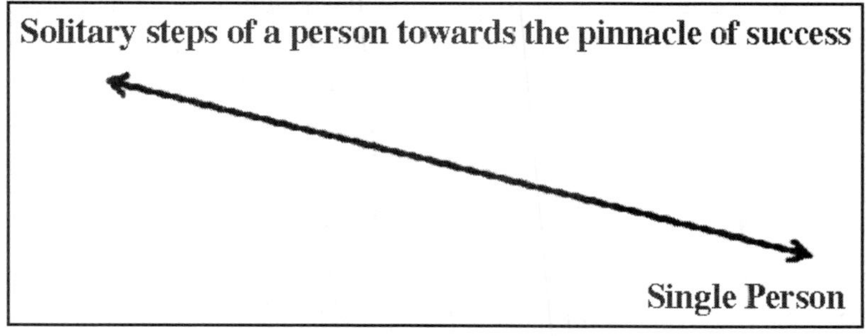

Lessons from Chanakya

A person who has resolved to march ahead alone is the strongest. Chanakya had braved many serious misfortunes and hardships during his childhood itself. He had endured the grief of his father's brutal murder and intolerable insults from people. Had he so wished, he could have withdrawn and quietly gone somewhere else. Instead, he resolved to fight the mountain-like obstacles all alone and he did succeed also. Chanakya used to say that an educated, prudent, honest and virtuous personality had the capacity to challenge history and even change the same. Of course, that single person has to be blessed with human values to accomplish the same.

❑

Nation First for a Human Being

Acharya's Pearls of Wisdom

- *Good people are known by their values.*
- *Nothing is impossible for a capable, deserving and courageous person.*
- *Every moment, prahar and day is extremely important. Hence, man should use them meaningfully.*

Nation First

Chanakya considered a conscientious, righteous, courageous ruler having leadership qualities as the best. He maintained that it was essential to develop good qualities in a person right from his very childhood. Childhood is soft phase like the clay on a potter's wheel. Hence, it can be moulded into desirable shapes. Chanakya had started training and equipping Chandragupta from his childhood itself for making him a noble and intelligent emperor. He wanted to present to the nation an emperor that did not deprive its people of their land, properties, right to livelihood, employment and other basic facilities while making plans for development. He used to even educate Chandragupta every now and then in this regard.

One day, after Chandragupta had been installed as emperor, Chanakya met him for some counselling and advice. After some chit-chat, he said, "Hey, tell me how is your plan for nation building progressing?"

Instead of responding to his query, Chanakya asked, "Okay, let me know where do you plan to establish the security infrastructure?"

Chandragupta was feeling a bit uneasy at Chanakya's annoyance and his endless questions. He said, "Acharya, that also is focussed on Magadha and its capital."

Chandragupta smiled and said, "Acharya, it's going on very well."

Finding Chandragupta smiling, Chanakya, taking his one hand below his chin, said, "Hmm! That's good. Can you let me know the details of expenses for nation building and also tell me where is the centre of such expenses?"

Chandragupta immediately got the details and placed the same before him. He said, "Acharya, the centre of expenses is our state Magadha and its capital Pataliputra."

Feeling a little confused, Chanakya asked, "Where do you plan to build schools and universities?"

Getting excited, Chandragupta replied, "We plan to build schools around Magadha and university in the capital to enable everybody in the state to get the best education."

The frowns on the forehead of Chanakya were clearly visible by the time Chandragupta finished his words. Sensing the same, Chandragupta asked, "Acharya, what's the matter?"

Instead of responding to his query, Chanakya asked, "Okay, let me know where do you plan to establish the security infrastructure?"

Chandragupta was feeling a bit uneasy at Chanakya's annoyance and his endless questions. He said, "Acharya, that also is focussed on Magadha and its capital."

Chanakya responded coolly, "People are living in this nation beyond Magadha and Pataliputra also. They also need everything. Are there any plans for those places beyond Magadha and the capital also?"

"Acharya, I believe everything would be okay once all facilities are available in the state and the capital."

Taking a deep breath, Chanakya said, "Keep this always in your mind that I have installed you not merely for the state of Magadha but also for the welfare of entire nation. You are just trying to fill up your own house by providing all facilities to Magadha and Pataliputra only. This should not happen. A country progresses when not only the ruler but also every person in that country thinks for the welfare of the nation and works towards nation building. Hence, you should formulate plans at the national level and build schools and universities across entire nation."

"Acharya, but as an emperor of Magadha, it's my prime responsibility to make my state and its capital the best," replied Chandragupta in a tempered voice.

Primarily responsibility for security of any nation lies with its armed forces. A member of armed forces is nation's guard first and a common citizen next. Chanakya's advice to nation's guards is that they should be strong and honest and should be always ready to risk their lives. A nation with such guards would never face any danger from enemies.

"Not at all. Making not only the state and its capital but also the entire nation the best is your supreme and first responsibility. It will be an indication of your narrow-mindedness if you focus only on the welfare of your state. If you wish to remain immortal in history, you need to only remember 'nation first, national interest foremost'. Chanakya was emphatic.

By now, Chandragupta had realised his mistake. "Acharya, I will always remember this and will always work towards national interest."

Chanakya agreed with him and went ahead to attend to his own jobs.

Nation Paramount For Soldiers

Primarily, responsibility for security of any nation lies with its armed forces. A member of armed forces is nation's guard first and a common citizen next. Chanakya's advice to nation's guards is that they should be strong and honest and should always be ready to risk their lives. A nation with such guards would never face any danger from enemies. Abhinandan Varthaman is one of such brave sons of India. He is a Wing Commander in Indian Air force. India had launched attack on Jaish location in Pakistan territory on 26 February 2019. Indian Air Force had dropped 1000 kg fusillade on terrorist camps of Jaish-e-Mohammed in Balakot. The news spread about many terrorists getting killed in this operation. India had used about 12 Mirage fighter jets for this assault. One of those MiG-21 jets was being flown by Wing Commander Abhinandan. He managed to shoot down one F-16 of Pakistan Air Force. Though F-16 is much better technically equipped, even it's power came a cropper in front of the courage and strength of brave Wing Commander Abhinandan. Abhinandan also got injured in the operation. He finally jumped off the jet with his parachute and landed in Pakistan territory.

He refused to divulge any classified information of India to the enemy country. The entire world hailed the bravery and courage of Wing Commander Abhinandan Varthaman and he was back in Indian territory safe and sound on 1 March 2019.

When he came to senses, he found a large crowd gathered around him. He checked with the people there if he was in India and also shouted 'Bharat Mata Ki Jai'. He could make out from the silence there that he was in enemy territory. Even at that moment, when he was in the custody of enemy forces and conditions were entirely inimical, he maintained his poise and acted in a brave and prudent manner. He refused to divulge any classified information of India to the enemy country. The entire world hailed the bravery and courage of Wing Commander Abhinandan Varthaman and he was back in Indian territory safe and sound on 1 March 2019.

Chanakya's ideas offered ages ago are found to be precisely true not only for rulers and soldiers but also for common people.

Chanakya's ideas offered ages ago are found to be precisely true not only for rulers and soldiers but also for common people.

National Interest Foremost for Citizens Also

Nation should come first in the heart of not only a ruler but also each of its citizens. People who value national interest become part of history and are remembered for ages. This is as true today as it was when Chanakya had said these words ages ago. A nation becomes great by welfare of its people, their deeds and their lifestyle. Hence, it is the duty of every citizen to realise his responsibility towards the interest of his nation. A citizen should ensure timely payment of his electricity and water bills in order to make the nation prosperous. Public properties should be kept clean. Taxes should be paid properly. Taxes should not be evaded. Tax evasion harms the nation a lot. The government uses these very tax collections for the provision of health, road and education facilities for people.

People should follow traffic rules when using roads. Innumerable accidents occur because of traffic rules violation. People should also ensure judicious utilisation of electricity and water in their homes so that these facilities could be distributed to all corners of the country. Many parts of Maharashtra and other states are still facing shortage of electricity and water. People at such places have to walk long distances to fetch a pitcher of water even today.

Basic facilities like electricity, water and housing can be made available to all if every citizen realises his responsibility properly.

Chanakya believed that progress of a nation depended on its ruler as well as its citizens. Hence, both should be honest and accountable to each other.

Role of Youth Towards Nation

Education facilitates all-round development of a person. Chanakya asserts that knowledge helps a person in fulfilling all his desires and in understanding properly his duties and responsibilities towards the welfare of the nation. Besides schools, if educated parents also help their children develop moral values right from their childhood, such children, while following the footsteps of their parents, become capable of forging their own path and march ahead towards nation building.

Education facilitates all-round development of a person. Chanakya asserts that knowledge helps a person in fulfilling all his desires and in understanding properly his duties and responsibilities towards the welfare of the nation. Besides schools, if educated parents also help their children develop moral values right from their childhood, such children, while following the footsteps of their parents, become capable of forging their own path and march ahead towards nation building. These days, we are coming across a number of youth who are busy making new inventions for the benefit of not only the nation but also for the common people.

One among such youth is Rifat Shahrukh of Tamilnadu. He has designed the world's smallest satellite. Named as Kalamsat,

Rifat Shahrukh' satellite was launched into the space in S.R.-4 rocket on 21 June 2017 from NASA facility in Wallops Island. The satellite has been named after great scientist Dr A. P. J. Abdul Kalam. His remarkable feat has made the entire world acknowledge India's calibre.

Anirudh Sharma is another such young inventor. He designed an innovative shoe 'LeChal' during the year 2010. 'LeChal' is a different kind of shoe. The mobile phone vibrator fitted inside the shoe helps a visually impaired person in navigating from one place to another. Not only this, he invented the 'Calink' technology for reducing pollution in the environment. This process absorbs carbon particles from a chimney or a diesel engine before the same get dispersed in the environment. This results in reduction in environmental pollution and at the same time, the polluting particles may be used for production of ink. 'Air-Ink' developed by Anirudh is being used in art, printing and fashion sectors.

Similarly, Nipun Goyal, a young electric engineer from IIT Delhi, has developed a mobile app named 'Curofy' through his own company with the same name 'Curofy'. This app helps doctors in better treatment of their patients by making available reliable information and materials. Students of Shavak Nanavati Technical Institute have developed eco-friendly bricks out of waste materials. These bricks are cheaper and more durable than traditional clay bricks. The brick is manufactured using fly ash, LD slag, waste materials from river pump houses, gypsum, lime powder and lime.

There are innumerable such youths who are today proving the words of Chanakya to be true. Chanakya not only gave the nation an able emperor during that ancient period but, it may also be clearly observed, his writings and lessons are even today playing an important role in making people virtuous and responsible citizens.

There are innumerable such youths who are today proving the words of Chanakya to be true. Chanakya not only gave the nation an able emperor during that ancient period but, it may also be clearly observed that his writings and lessons are even today playing an important role in making people virtuous and responsible citizens.

Following Steps Necessary in National Interest

Chanakya believed that every child who was taught lessons on righteousness, respect for elders etc. from the very childhood bloomed from a bud to a full-grown flower as a mentally strong person. Following steps should definitely be taken in every country in the national interest.

Education - Knowledge is revered everywhere in the world. A person may make not only his country but also the entire universe recognise his talent on the strength of his education. A well-educated person, blessed with moral values, thinks in the national interest.

*Every moment, **prahar** and day of life is very important. Hence, man should use the same meaningfully. Every person should realise his duty and responsibility and work for the interest of the nation to ensure its continuous development and to preserve its prosperity and well-being.*

Building High Quality Schools and Universities - It's essential for a country to have the best of schools and universities. It's very necessary to build universities where everybody may have access to education without any bias of his caste or class. A person after getting educated as per his abilities becomes ready for nation building.

Strong Security System - It's essential for the security system of a country to be strong. Enemy forces launched an inhuman assault on Indian soldiers posted in Uri area of Jammu &

Kashmir on 18 September 2016. Similarly, the attack in Pulwama of Jammu & Kashmir on 14 February 2019 stirred the heart of every Indian. Hence, strategies should be developed with reason and prudence so that enemies do not get any chance to breach the security network.

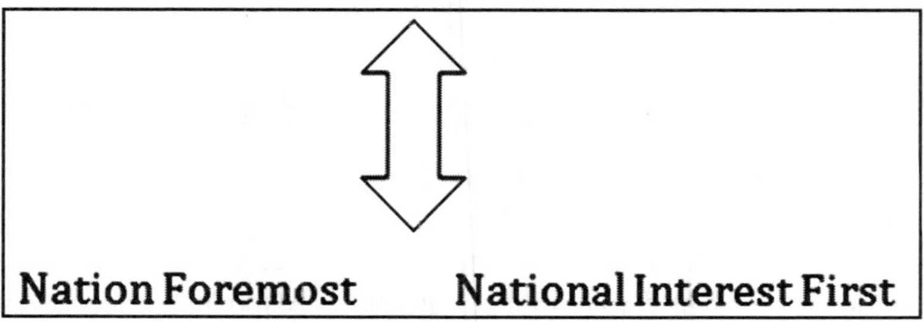

Lessons from Chanakya

Every moment, prahar and day of life is very important. Hence, man should use the same meaningfully. Every person should realise his duty and responsibility and work for the interest of the nation to ensure its continuous development and to preserve its prosperity and well-being. It is important to develop the sense of patriotism and feeling of complete dedication towards homeland in the conscience of every person from his very childhood. When everybody fulfils his duty towards his country properly, the country marches ahead on the path of development and creates new records every day.

❑

A Treatise on Finance

Acharya's Pearls of Wisdom

- *Accumulation of wealth reflects a person's intelligence.*
- *Wealth acquired by honest means stays with the person for entire life and it keeps on growing constantly.*
- *Usage of wealth increases its importance.*

Economics

'Artha' means wealth, money or finance and 'shastra' refers to a treatise. Thus, the primary meaning of 'Arthashastra' authored by Chanakya, also identified as Kautilya, is a treatise on finance. Credit for successful management of economics in India goes to Chanakya only. Every student used to be highly impressed by the lessons taught by Chanakya. Once, some of his students said to him, "Acharya, after you, nobody would be able to enlighten students on economics and life so nicely with such expertise. Thus, your knowledge would go with you."

After getting similar remarks from many students, Chanakya decided to put his knowledge into black and white and started his writing work. The *Arthashastra* not only explains finance related ideas with expertise but also covers information related to politics, society, wisdom, science and all other areas.

We now and then come across people around us who believe that it's foolish to accumulate wealth. They accept that only rich people have right over wealth and they keep on blaming sometime the economy and some other time the policies for their own poverty. However, the truth remains that nobody else but the person himself is the biggest cause for his poverty.

Chanakya has organised his entire work in 15 books and 150 chapters. The entire treatise has around 5000 sutras. These sutras are capable of conveying ideas on all aspects like life, philosophy, politics, society, finance and checks and balances. Economists and philosophers of the world have acknowledged the greatness of the Arthashastra and recognised the same as an extremely valuable scripture for the world. All areas of modern economics viz. microeconomics, macroeconomics, rules for auditing, tax and penalty procedures, condition of women, religion and politics, caste system, duties of a ruler, duties of citizens, etc. have been explained in minute details in the *Arthashastra*.

Complete Meanings of '*Nirdhan*' and Poor

Chanakya has emphasised the importance of wealth very sensibly. He does accept wealth as essential for living, but he also mentions that 'excessive accumulation of wealth not only corrupts the mind of a person, it also makes him greedy and selfish.' Hence, man should accumulate wealth using his intelligence and ability through honest means only. A very old maxim is quite popular even today that goddess Saraswati and goddess Lakshmi can't go together. However, Chanakya did not agree to the same as he himself had used his knowledge to make Chandragupta an emperor. Not only that, he could have enjoyed all kinds of luxury had he so wished but he had decided of his own free will to lead a simple life. He who acquires knowledge wholeheartedly can very well earn money also. Where there is Saraswati, Lakshmi has to come, as Saraswati is the goddess of knowledge, art and wisdom.

We now and then come across people around us who believe that it's foolish to accumulate wealth. They accept that only rich people have right over wealth and they keep on blaming sometime the economy and some other time the policies for their own poverty. However, the truth remains that nobody else but the person himself is the biggest cause for his poverty.

The equivalent English word for 'Nirdhan' is 'POOR'. Do you know what could be the full form of POOR? The word may be expanded as - Passing Over Opportunities Regularly.

Similarly, 'Nirdhan' may be interpreted as 'Nirantar Dhan Nahin' meaning 'Constantly without wealth'.

Thus, both English and Hindi words 'Poor' and 'Nirdhan' in their full form indicate lack of wealth for a person and also convey that the person is poor because of his own foolishness and inability.

Sethji was quite impressed by his words. He not only purchased fruits from him but, finding him to be so clever and intelligent, also arranged for his studies and started to give him lessons on the secrets of business. He was already in search of such a clever boy only for his business.

World famous billionaire Bill Gates fully agrees to the above concept when he says that 'if you are born poor, it's not your mistake, but if you die poor, it's your mistake'.

Chanakya asserts that 'a person should definitely accumulate wealth to avoid miseries for himself.'

Here is a typical story.

Two boys were selling fruits sitting close to each other. Both had stacks of sweet fruits. No customer had come to them for buying fruits since morning. Suddenly, they found one clever wealthy businessman coming towards them. Seeing him, the first boy called out, "Sethji, buy some sweet fruits please!"

Sethji did not pay attention to the boy and walked ahead. The second boy then came to him and said, "Sethji, it's my birthday today. You are the 50th person to pass by my stall. I had already decided that I would give my delicious fruits to the 50th person passing by my stall free of cost and make my birthday meaningful and memorable. Please have these fruits."

Sethji was quite impressed by his words. He not only purchased fruits from him but, finding him to be so clever and intelligent, also arranged for his studies and started to give him lessons on the secrets of business. He was already in search of such a clever boy for his business.

Villages - the Primary Source of Wealth for a Country

Better natural resources would make the agricultural system of the country better. Agriculture and farmers not only strengthen the economy of the country but also make the monetary policies of India powerful. Chanakya believed that the wealth should be used prudently. The entire country, including even remote villages and farmers, should not experience any kind of scarcity.

Chanakya, in Chapter 14 of Book 7 of his *Arthashastra*, mentions that wealth and power come primarily from rural areas. The rural areas only have the resources that mainly activate all the development. An analysis of economy of any developed country makes it clear that all the natural resources are located in rural areas only. The lifestyle of metro cities is quite busy and polluted.

The life there is full of glitter and luxuries but is quite busy and there is paucity of time. Natural resources are fast depleting. If we have to strengthen the economy of our country, it is necessary that we develop all our towns, villages and backward regions. Chanakya insists that it is the duty of a ruler to be committed to the development of villages. Today, many schemes are being implemented for development of villages like Saansad Adarsh Gram Yojana, Smart City, pucca roads, electricity to all homes and construction of toilets. Once basic facilities like electricity, water and toilets are provided and pucca roads are built there, the villages would be able to function smoothly and production of natural resources would improve greatly. Better natural resources would make the agricultural system of the country better. Agriculture and agriculturists are the backbone of society as they not only strengthen the economy of the country but also make the monetary policies of India powerful. Chanakya believed that the wealth should be used prudently. The entire country, including even remote villages and farmers, should not experience any kind of scarcity.

Proper Usage of Natural Resources Augments Wealth

The prosperity of any nation is reflected in quality of life, education, happiness and health of its residents. If only a few in a country are affluent and wealthy and most of the people there are living below poverty line, the country would be known as a poor nation only. In order to bring about equality in income for all, it is necessary that everybody in the country gets equal opportunity of education and development. Besides this, people should ensure that natural resources are utilised prudently. Indiscriminate usage of natural resources impacts the economic potential of a country. Chanakya maintains that the responsibility of strengthening the economy of a country should lie with both its ruler and its people. The basic facilities like electricity and water should be used in limited quantities in order to make the same available for all in equal amounts. People would be more productive when they have uniform access to natural resources. Both overuse and underuse of natural resources by people impact the power of economy.

Wealth Policy

Why is it so that one person is poor while the other is affluent? The *Arthashastra* and *Chanakya Niti* state that wealth is the true friend of a man. It's only wealth that comes to the rescue of a person in the case of a calamity and a disaster. In fact, economic policy plays an important role in making people rich or poor. Chanakya has formulated many schemes for ensuring effectiveness of policies relating to economy as well as all other endeavours. Those schemes are aimed to make people prosperous, affluent and happy.

As per second policy of wealth, people should indulge less in complaining and more in work. Quite often, people spend most of their valuable time in blaming others and making complaints against them. Besides wastage of time, complaints bring with them tension also.

Wealth policies indicate that the person who has the desire to be affluent and prosperous never blames others or his fate for his condition, rather takes all the responsibility for his shortcomings that are preventing him to succeed. If the person with all sincerity tries to find out those shortcomings, he soon gets to know his mistakes. He then corrects those mistakes and moves ahead and thus, learns the first lesson of economics that a person should take responsibility for all his actions. Delegating entire responsibility for a job to somebody else has the possibility of deceit by that person. Similarly, fate is just another form of the hard work of a person. The more is your effort and hard work, the more is your affluence and opulence.

As per second policy of wealth, people should indulge less in complaining and more in work. Quite often, people spend most of their valuable time in blaming others and making complaints against them. Besides wastage of time, complaints bring with them tension also. A tense brain can't work with an open mind and our brain is just like a parachute that works only when fully open. Fights and complaints many a time get very nasty and result in substantial damage to the person.

You may very well make out from the above that a person should embrace the policy of 'Forget complaints, focus on work and surmount every obstacle' for wealth creation.

The third policy of wealth says that a person should keep on experimenting. Nowadays, we often observe that many innovations aimed towards modernisation and common good, not only earn name and fame for the concerned person but also provide him the greatest power to acquire wealth. Experimentation only helped Ruth Handler create Barbie Dolls. Many people made fun of her for her experiment to launch a doll in the market, but she just ignored them. Barbie Doll was eventually very successful in the market. Mattel went on to grow to be the largest producer of toys in the United States of America on the strength of this very doll. Not only that, Barbie Doll also helped Mattel get the golden opportunity of being included in 'Fortune 500' list.

It was their devoutness for experimentation only that helped Bloomberg, Howard Schultz, Larry Page and Sergey Brin acquire wealth as well as earn name and fame.

Just as gold gets refined by going through heating and melting, a positive and honest person remains true to his moral values even in the midst of people with doubtful characters and judgemental attitude. Such people progress with more speed and vigour and successfully acquire wealth.

The fourth policy of wealth is that a person should always remain positive. Positive thoughts infuse people with energy. A person filled with energy and self-confidence possesses the power to eliminate the darkness and bring about the brightness of sunshine. Hunger, poverty, fights exist more in the state of darkness. A zestful person knows how to stop a storm, how to break a large rock and how to make his way through hurricanes. Such a person remains positive and active even in the midst of negative people and unfavourable circumstances. Just as gold gets refined by going through heating and melting, a positive and honest person remains true to his moral values even in the midst of people with doubtful characters and judgemental attitude. Such people progress with more speed and vigour and successfully acquire wealth.

Wealth Policies

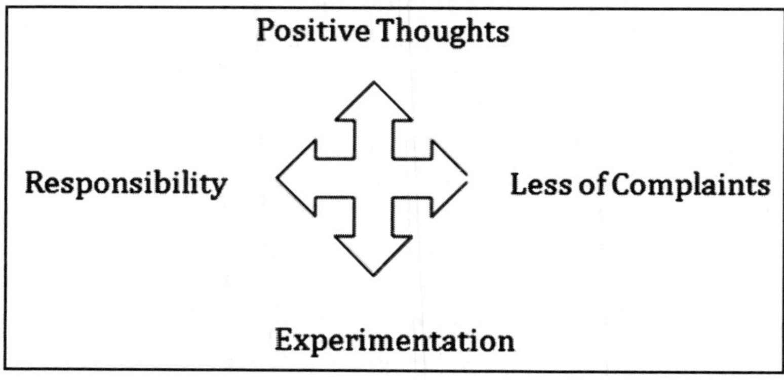

Lessons from Chanakya

All the pleasures are available to a person who possesses wealth. The power of wealth is very forceful. Even a foe becomes a friend and a friend becomes a foe under the influence of money. However, wealth should be always acquired using proper means. Only the wealth acquired with honesty, intelligence and adroitness helps a person grow. The wealth acquired by means of theft, deceit and immoral activities is worthless. Such wealth can never provide peace, pleasure and happiness to a person. Wealthy and affluent persons should donate money to the needy and the poor. If a person makes use of his wealth for endeavours meant for common good, he becomes immortal. Daanaveer Karna, demon king Bali and Vikramaditya became world famous as they gave away their own wealth to the needy. A ruler should ensure development of villages and remote areas for economic development of the country. It's also necessary to ensure proper usage of natural resources. They augment the wealth and happiness for both the country and its people.

❑

Enriched Lifestyle of Chanakya

Acharya's Pearls of Wisdom

- *Fate rewards a person as per his deeds.*
- *A man's personality is a reflection of his entire expressive style.*
- *Compassion removes all the fears of a person.*
- *Well-cultured and prudent persons bravely face difficult situations, as they are capable of enduring adverse circumstances.*

Lifestyle

The personal preferences and behaviour with which an individual spends his life is called his lifestyle. Lifestyle mostly depends on environment and situations but spirited, well-cultured and prudent persons are capable of braving all kinds of adverse circumstances.

They do not get carried away by such adverse situations, instead they successfully fight and turn the tide of such adverse situations. On the other hand, weak-kneed persons get shaken up even with minor adversities and sit quiet giving up the struggle. They are not able to make out how to take their lives out of such situations. Such people just keep floating with the flow of adverse conditions. In such situations, their lifestyles keep bending as per the environment, as they do not apply their mind. They also do not possess the will power to understand that adverse conditions may only threaten them for a short while but can't stop them from reaching their destinations. While giving lessons to his students, Chanakya would often tell them about practical lifestyle. He believed in making the foundation of their students strong from the very beginning. Once, two of his students were assigned responsibility of a job. Both of them failed to complete the job. When Chanakya asked them the reason for not doing the job, they started blaming each other. Chanakya then said, "Just keep this in mind! The person who tries to blame others for hiding his own mistakes would never be able to have the courage to move ahead alone, as he would be always looking for somebody who could be blamed for his failures."

The students promptly responded, "No, no! We don't want to fail in our lives. We have to succeed."

"That's correct! But for that, you must always remember that nobody else but you only would have to take yourself to your goal. Hence, be always alert, energetic and righteous."

The students assured him to follow his advice.

Life as a School

Life is a school. Right from the birth until his last breath, the process of learning for a person is constantly in progress. One who stops learning becomes stagnant. The stagnant water in a lake does not flow and hence rots and stinks. The individuals who do not have any yearning desire to progress in their lives and do not nurture any aim in their minds also, and just like that stagnant water in a lake, create problems for others after some time because of their existence. Progress is the law of life. One who is static is dead. A dead person or thing exits this life. A person, thing, creature or living being who does not have anything to give and who is not able to do anything is as good as dead. The 'Dead Sea' of Jordon is called 'dead' sea because of its high salinity that makes it's water unfit for any use. Nobody would be interested to see anything or any creature that has no utility on this earth. The warp and weft and the fabric of society is created in a way such that nobody gives any importance to the people who are worthless. Such people always fail in the school of life. Chanakya points out that life teaches many lessons to a person. He encounters many kinds of experiences right from his childhood up to old age. Those experiences should be shared with others to help coming generations reap benefits from the same and progress towards a prosperous lifestyle. Not only the self-development but also all round development is essential for progress towards a prosperous lifestyle.

Life is a school. Right from birth until his last breath, the process of learning for a person is constantly in progress. One who stops learning becomes stagnant. The stagnant water in a lake does not flow and hence rots and stinks. The individuals who do not have any yearning desire to progress in their lives and do not nurture any aim in their minds also, just like that stagnant water in a lake, create problems for others after some time because of their existence.

Chanakya's Experiences

Chanakya was learned and knowledgeable and blessed with an eye for talent. He had encountered so many people in his life that he had become a mobile thesaurus for definitions and interpretations for prosperous lifestyle and good and bad life. All students and even common people would go to him for finding solutions to their problems. And Chanakya's solutions would be so precise that they would resolve the problems without any harm to anyone. Many of the Acharyas at the Gurukula were very impressed by Chanakya for his erudition. One day, Chanakya was working on some teaching materials for coming generations and was just lost in thought when a senior Acharya came to him and asked, "Chanakya, where are you lost?"

Chanakya said, "I have seen the best and the worst in my life. In fact, those experiences of life have taught me a lot."

Death is certain on this earth. But, I am aware of the fact that a person like you had never been there before and would never be there again on this earth. Your profound knowledge, prudence, intelligence and the art of living transformed a an ordinary boy into Emperor Chandragupta.

"Chanakya, this life is mortal. Death is certain on this earth. But, I am aware of the fact that a person like you never existed before and would never be there again on this earth. Your profound knowledge, prudence, intelligence and the art of living transformed an ordinary boy into Emperor Chandragupta. This makes us feel that coming generations who take lessons from you would be able not only to enrich their own lifestyles but also make their families and country proud with their high standard of living."

Chanakya looked towards that senior Acharya and asked, "What exactly are you trying to say?"

"What I am trying to convey is that you should pen your experiences and compile a book."

Chanakya responded with a smile, "This is certainly a very relevant point you have mentioned. Now even I am feeling too eager to write that book."

"Then why delay this auspicious work? Take your pen and start giving form to that great treatise on attaining the best quality of life."

This is how Chanakya created the *Arthashastra*.

Chanakya gives due importance to advanced lifestyle. An advanced lifestyle does not indicate abundance of money and wealth, rather it refers to the level of satisfaction that the person has in respect of love for his own self.

Even today the *Arthashastra* is considered to be the best treatise for reflection and contemplation not only on politics but also on economics and life. The work appears to be as relevant today as it was ages ago when it had been authored. This is so because Chanakya has elucidated many of the natural subtleties and perceptions of life in his work. In this modern age, man may surely adapt to the modern lifestyle but he cannot get rid of his basic tendencies. Thus, the *Arthashastra* guides every person to attain a happy and prosperous life. Even the western thinkers agree to the idea of quality of life propounded by Chanakya.

Advanced Lifestyle

Chanakya gives due importance to advanced lifestyle. An advanced lifestyle does not indicate abundance of money and wealth, rather it refers to the level of satisfaction that the person has in respect of love for his own self. You just try to figure out in your heart whether you would really like your own self if you happen to meet him in his real form. If the answer is yes, it means that you have the attributes for developing advanced lifestyle along with the ability to live according to the same. When every day of life provides joy of living, it indicates an advanced lifestyle. People who always keep bemoaning for their problems are able to neither find solution to their problems nor develop their lifestyles appropriately. A proper and advanced lifestyle fills all the gaps and makes the life of a person joyful.

Enriched Lifestyle

Chanakya makes it clear in the *Arthashastra* and the *Chanakya Niti* that people should not indulge in only acquiring wealth but also in understanding the best way to live.

Some people, despite being surrounded by infinitely beautiful things do not feel happiness in their hearts whereas there are also people who are blessed with unlimited wealth but their minds and hearts remain plagued by constant worries and anxious thoughts. Some people, despite being extraordinarily rich are empty-hearted and at the same time, there are also people who are not blessed with too much of wealth but they always feel contented and live a good life.

Here, giving does not refer only to material helps or gifts; rather, it may be in any form. Though, of course, when you offer help, you should do the same with complete selflessness and to an extent a little more than what you would have originally thought. That little extra help over your original idea would provide you a feeling of richness for the whole day.

The best way to attain an enriched lifestyle is to keep on draining accumulated wealth through gifts and donations. While such a person earns name The glitter of his self-confidence starts getting reflected on his face. His face shines with enthusiasm. A good lifestyle also means that the person should reward every excellence. Every time he rewards an excellence, he himself also gets rewarded. All this enriches his lifestyle and provides him a superior and successful life.

Here, giving does not refer only to material helps or gifts; rather, it may be in any form. Though, of course, when you offer help, you should do the same with complete selflessness and to an extent a little more than what you would have originally thought. That little extra help over your original idea would provide you a feeling of richness for the whole day.

Just imagine you are travelling in a car. The car stops at a traffic signal. A girl aged around 15 years comes to your car. She is holding many colourful balloons in her hand. She tries to sell them to you. You agree to buy 10 balloons and ask her for the price. She enthusiastically tells you the price as Rs 100 only. You take out Rs 110 from your pocket and hand over the same to the girl. Getting 110 instead of 100 rupees, her eyes glitters with excitement and she thanks you wholeheartedly. By then the signal turns green and your car moves ahead, but after this, you too feel your heart brimming with self-satisfaction, self-confidence and happiness. For the whole day, you feel yourself to be affluent and self-confident. That petty amount of Rs 10 offered extra makes the psyche of the person soar significantly thus helping to make his lifestyle matured and enriched.

In order to attain a enriched lifestyle, the above should be definitely done in all such cases where the receiver is genuinely needy, noble and hard-working.

If a person attains proficiency in the art of lifestyle and pleasure, ampleness of wealth enhances his happiness and internal riches. The glitter of his self-confidence starts getting reflected on his face. His face shines with enthusiasm. A good lifestyle also means that the person should reward every excellence. Every time he rewards an excellence, he himself also gets rewarded. All this enriches his lifestyle and provides him a superior and successful life.

Prosperous Lifestyle

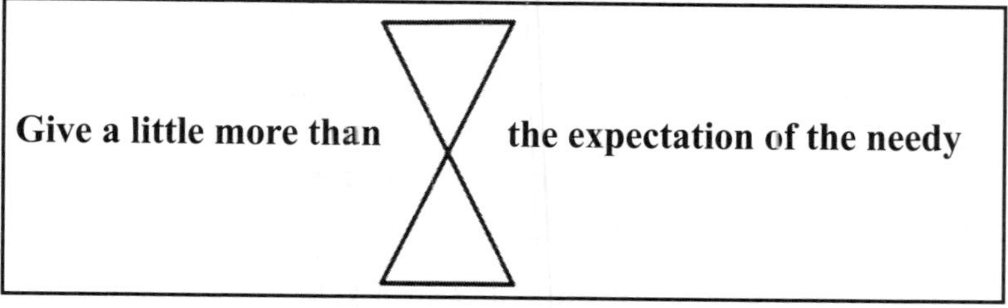

Lessons from Chanakya

Life is a school. A person should keep learning something new every day in the same. One who performs karma and toils every day is constantly on the path of success. Man is a social animal. Feelings and life values are always present in him. Hence, every living being should definitely help needy persons and living beings. Only the person who open-heartedly lends a helping hand to helpless people enjoys an enriched lifestyle. Having an enriched lifestyle does not mean just accumulating luxuries for self only, rather it also entails providing means of pleasure and happiness to people with comparatively lower status and make their drooping faces bloom like flowers. When a person helps others with open heart or appreciates others without any inhibition, a seed of self-confidence, peace and happiness starts germinating in his inner self. Buds of such mature persons attract everybody. As far as possible, people should keep helping each other with selflessness.

❑

Kavi - Ravi

Acharya's Pearls of Wisdom

- *As a man sows so he reaps. A person's deeds, good or bad, dictate the consequences he has to face.*
- *A happy life free from suffering and troubles is attained on the strength of good deeds.*
- *A person who acquires knowledge definitely gets all his desires fulfilled.*
- *Intelligence, prudence and values of even an unattractive person eliminate all the hurdles in his path to progress.*

Meaning of Kavi-Ravi

Chanakya usually knew the differences between obscure words and their meanings. He himself was an excellent writer. He had met innumerable persons in his lifetime and that had made him well conscious of the good and the bad. He would often amaze his students by revealing to them some unique ways of managing challenges and hurdles.

Once, Chanakya was busy with some writing job in the Gurukula. He had already assigned tasks to his students to memorise lessons and had also instructed them to get in touch with him immediately if any of them had any doubt or problem in understanding any lesson.

A young student saw the words 'Kavi-Ravi' in his lesson. What's the connection of Kavi (poet) with Ravi (the Sun)? He further read, 'जहाँ ना पहुँचे रवि, वहाँ पहुँचे कवि (Where the Sun cannot reach, the poet will reach)'. Even after going through the same 2-3 times, the student could not clear his doubt. He then approached Chanakya. Finding the student deep in thoughts, Chanakya asked, "What happened? Is everything alright?"

The student said, "Where the Sun cannot reach, the poet will reach. Is a poet's inspiring vision really so spirited? Kindly clarify."

"This is a very good question. Let all the students assemble before I explain."

Very soon, all the students assembled around Chanakya. Chanakya said, "A poet is very far-sighted. His connoisseur's eyes are able to easily grasp the happenings all around the world. Many a time, he is even aware of the consequences. At the time of Mahabharata, Vyas knew that if at all the war of Mahabharata did take place, the same would destroy everything and the entire human race would be in danger, and that's what actually happened."

"Acharya, but how is that possible? Does a poet or a writer possess divine vision?"

Where there is darkness, there are problems, worries and distress. The light of the Sun resolves many of the problems entangled in darkness. But, how to remove darkness from the places where even the light of the Sun does not reach? Who is capable of removing darkness from those places? A poet removes darkness from such places.

"You may treat it to be so. A person engrossed in writing does possess divine and unique vision. And if that is combined with knowledge, the same attains excellence. Knowledge is such a precious jewel that makes the vision of a person far-sighted and extraordinary. After all, our ancestors would not have said this without any purpose 'Where the Sun cannot reach, the poet will reach'."

This centuries-old maxim conceals a very emotional and abstruse meaning.

Where there is darkness, there are problems, worries and distress. The light of the Sun resolves many of the problems concealed in darkness. But, how to remove darkness from the places where even the light of the Sun does not reach? Who is capable of removing darkness from those places? A poet removes darkness from such places.

The literature of Kabir and Premchand looks fresh even today. A poet's connoisseur's eyes are able to sense the things to come in the future.

Richard Douglas Fosbury used the self-devised step for high jump competitions. His step used for high jump is so popular today that the same is known as 'Fosbury Flop'.

The word 'Kavi' means **Ka**rma + ***Vi***dya (Knowledge).

A person who is busy in acquiring knowledge discovers himself, his universe and his history. Of course, such a person should surely have some goals for common good. Learning exposes better angels of a person. Books play a decisive role in building the future of a person. They are friends to him forever and they keep him guiding to the right direction. He, who knows learning, is aware of the power to develop himself, to enrich his lifestyle in various ways and to make his life complete, meaningful and pleasant. If a person busy in studying is also hardworking, it just exemplifies the saying 'icing on the cake'. Such a person not only earns name, fame and prosperity but also inspires many others after he is gone. The person who believes in both knowledge and karma busts many myths, creates history and sets a new example.

Hollywood actor Hedy Lamarr, Richard Douglas Fosbury, Oseola McCarty and Walter Scott are examples of such personalities only who made their own lives meaningful on the strength of 'Kavi' i.e. karma and knowledge. Hollywood actor Hedy Lamarr, making a splash in the field of inventions besides her acting, has proved that when a person has passion and yearning, he may, despite being in a field of glamour, use his knowledge to set new records even in the field of inventions. Richard Douglas Fosbury used the self-devised step for high jump competitions. His step used for high jump is so popular today that the same is known as 'Fosbury Flop'. Similarly, Oseola McCarty could not get formal education because of circumstances but she worked hard against all odds and donated her entire savings to the University of Southern Mississippi to provide scholarships to economically weaker African-American students and help them build great future for themselves. In the same way, Walter Scott grew to be a world famous litterateur because of his interest in literature from his very childhood.

Whereeven the Sun is unable to reach, a person shines like the Sun after surmounting all hurdles with the union of karma and knowledge. No darkness can stand up to an individual when his personality gets the brightness of the Sun. Ravi (the Sun) also conceals a deep meaning within itself.

Ravi = '**ra**ch' + '**vi**patti' ('create' + 'adversity').

Ravi means the Sun ('dinakar', 'bhaskar', 'martandeya'). When soft and mellow rays of the Sun come out of the gaps of the mountains at the down of the day, the darkness vanishes. Even a single soft ray of light is enough to brighten total darkness. It is well known that when the Sun rises, darkness vanishes. The deeper meaning of Ravi is 'rach' + 'vipatti'.

The famous research scientist Charles F. Kattering was a philosopher and an inventor of the highest order. He used to tell people to bring to him more and more of problems as the problems always made him strong and augmented the productivity of his brain.

People on this earth are certainly making a lot of progress but even today, many issues and practices are just being followed as a matter of tradition. People don't try to deviate from those traditions and when anybody does look beyond those traditions, he brightens up his entire life with pure light.

There is a common psychological feeling that adversities upset people, disrupt their lives and make their path rugged and rocky. However, this is only an illusion. This illusion conceals a gold-like brightness and unlimited success. Many of the philosophers agree and believe that every adversity brings with it great opportunities and adversities prove to be the decisive points for the best performance for a person. Hence, you should be ready to brave the problems and hurdles. The famous research scientist Charles F. Kattering was a philosopher and an inventor of the highest order. He used to tell people to bring to him more and more of problems as the problems always made him strong and augmented the productivity of his brain.

Thus, the Sun, with his other name Ravi, conveys the message to people to 'create adversities' ('rach' + 'vipatti') and sharpen 'mati'. 'Mati' i.e. intelligence of a person improves when he contemplates facing up to his problems. When he thinks, his inventiveness reaches its peak and he is led to the path of innovations. Hence, you should focus on 'Ravi-Kavi' and create new path everyday for refinement. Doing that helps a person get a feeling of self-satisfaction.

If you have a feeling of 'Ravi' in your inner-self, i.e. you know how to find your way out of the adversities, it's a matter of great satisfaction. However, even if it's not the case, you should not get worried; rather you should take 'Kavi' along with you, that is to say, you sincerely acquire knowledge and follow the path of karma. By doing that, you would be both 'Ravi' and 'Kavi' and surmount all the hurdles and difficulties on the strength of your knowledge.

Created Opportunities Out of Adversities

*The **Arthashastra** of Chanakya guides not only the leaders but also the ordinary people today and helps them understand that even the severest of adversities brings with it great opportunities. Knowledge and positive wisdom never allow a person either to surrender or to lose his will power. Hence, just remember **Ravi-Kavi** along with Chanakya Niti and march ahead on your path relentlessly.*

Chanakya was extraordinary. There was no limit to his intelligence. He had gone through a life full of adversities. He had endured the pain of his father's death and had seen the immoral and brutal atrocities of Dhananand in Pataliputra. After encountering so many severe adversities, he had started to find new opportunities and new ways in them. He himself was not in a position to become an emperor. Though his horoscope had the combinations indicating the possibility of his becoming a famous emperor, he had, out of his love for his mother, removed all those of his teeth that reflected the signs of an emperor.

Chanakya's father was also a teacher and he had to meet a painful death only because of his opposition to the atrocities of Dhanananda. Death of his father had compelled him to look for a person who was extraordinary and was capable of making India immortal on the strength of his personality. He discovered Chandragupta, groomed him as an emperor and pitted him against Dhanananda. He was successful in wiping out the entire family of Dhanananda and installing Chandragupta as the emperor. Thus, he was also known as an emperor-maker. Many of the rulers were committed to his *Nitishastra* and his policies. The *Arthashastra* of Chanakya guides not only the leaders but also the ordinary people today and helps them understand that even the severest of adversities brings with it great opportunities. Knowledge and positive wisdom never allow a person either to surrender or to lose his will power. Hence, just remember Ravi-Kavi along with Chanakya Niti and march ahead on your path relentlessly.

Resolve and Perfect Ravi-Kavi

Chanakya maintains that if a person decides on a plan of action based on his convenience and the surroundings and then moves ahead, he may attain his desired goals. While 'Ravi' refers to 'rach' + 'vipatti' ('create' + 'adversity'), the person may also interpret 'Kavi' as 'kal' + 'vijeta' ('tomorrow' + 'winner') as per his convenience. A person who does not succumb to an adverse situation today goes on to be a winner tomorrow for sure. Every calamity and every adversity can be overcome with a strong determination.

Lessons from Acharya

An intelligent and prudent person knows how to control his senses with concentration. He is aware of the fact that adversities, fresh and great opportunities always come disguised with obstacles and problems. Hence he welcomes trivial problems and in the case of a big problem, he is ready to welcome and confront the same with double the enthusiasm. Adversities in a way indicate the speed of growth. It may be a matter of concern if problems and obstacles are not encountered on this path of progress, as there is only one place on this earth where a person does not have to face any adversity or problem. That place is the graveyard or the cremation ground. The dead man is buried there. No obstacle exists for a dead person. The obstacles are there only when there is life. Hence, brave every obstacle and adversity treating the same as a great challenge. A person having positive thoughts, knowledge, prudence and courage can rip up any adversity and come out successfully. The personalities of those people only who are capable of conquering adversities glow with fame.

❑

Threads and Forms of Everlasting Friendship

Acharya's Pearls of Wisdom

- *The friendship between two persons would be everlasting only when there is a union of their minds, their deepest thoughts and their intelligence.*
- *A trustworthy person only can be a true friend.*
- *Only a person, who behaves as a friend despite being not related, should be considered a true friend, companion, support and reliance.*
- *One who stands by in happiness as well as in distress is a true friend.*

What is Friendship?

Friendship between Krishna and Sudama of the mythological era is even today considered to be an example not only for friends but also for the entire world. Krishna never presented himself as an emperor in front of his poor friend Sudama. He always looked for the glimpse of simplicity and naughtiness of childhood in Sudama.

Chanakya believed that only a trustworthy person could be a true friend.

Whereas Chanakya considers friends to be necessary for living, he also mentions that one should be extremely careful while making friends and while sharing secrets with them. Just an acquaintance with a person is not a friendship. These days, people get acquainted with each other easily through Facebook, Whatsapp, Instagram, Twitter and other social media platforms and they treat those casual acquaintances as friendship. A friendship is not just an acquaintance. Friendship is in fact such a beautiful relationship of life that is capable of giving rise to all other kinds of love in the heart of a person. Lord Jesus had given a lot of importance to relationships. There are many instances in His sayings also where He has laid emphasis on friendship. He believed that when people become friends with purity in their hearts, their inner selves spontaneously start swinging with feelings of love. When a feeling of love gets kindled in the heart of a person, he starts getting rid of many vices. In friendship, people share their thoughts with each other and clear confusions in their minds. The relationship of friendship is the most unique, amazing and fascinating. The bonding of a friendship is neither based on any blood relationship nor any alliance, rather it is related to union of hearts. A person chooses his friends without any constraint. Friendship does not differentiate on the basis of sex, age, religion or caste.

Friendship between Krishna and Sudama of the mythological era is considered even today to be an example not only for friends but also for the entire world. Krishna never presented himself as an emperor in front of his poor friend Sudama. He always looked for the glimpse of simplicity and naughtiness of childhood in Sudama.

Chanakya believed that only a trustworthy person could be a true friend.

Threads of Deep Friendship

People create a society. People have to anyhow depend on each other for their livelihood. A person in need or in trouble gets the best support from a true friend only.

- **Union of Minds and Brains of Friends**: Chanakya asserts that a friendship between two persons can be firm only when there is a union of their minds, their brains and their deepest thoughts. It's common for close friends to perceive the grief or happiness of each other without the need for a word. They are able to figure out everything just by signs and expression. It is essential for the friends to understand the feelings of each other and remain sincere to each other to make their friendship ever-lasting.
- **Friendly Behaviour with Trust and Honesty:** Only he is a true friend who always wishes growth, happiness, good health and peace for his friend. Chanakya says that the person who behaves like a friend even though not related, is a true friend, companion, support and reliance. A successful friend always stands by his dear ones and offers full support for their growth and development. Relationship is not significant in a friendship. Even without any relationship, a person bonds with his friend to the extent that he is unable to conceive his life without that friend. Friendship does not make any differentiation on the basis of age, sex and religion. Not only that, he devotes his entire life to his friend.

- In this Kalayuga also, many examples of fast friendship can be found depicting rare instances of extraordinary camaraderie even in the absence of any relationship.
- It was spring of 1887. The Nature was in full bloom. Amaltas, palash, gulmohar, rose, chrysanthemum, xenia, dahlia, salvia and innumerable other flowers appeared to be smiling on their freshness and dancing in excitement. Trees also looked to be swinging in gay abundance with green and yellow crowns on their heads and welcoming every visitor. At that very time, a 20-years old young lady arrived in Alabama. She had come there to work as a teacher for a blind and deaf girl. Her name was Annie Sullivan and the blind and deaf girl was Helen Keller. They were not related initially, but gradually they came so close to each other that they just changed the history. Their friendship became a unique example of the century.
- Helen Keller was just one-and-a-half years old when she got ill with high fever. This illness left her blind, deaf and dumb. She could not speak at all up to the age of seven. When angry and agitated, she would throw stuff here and there and cry out loudly. Such behaviour of innocent Helen even prompted people to comment to her mother that she had given birth to a brainless and useless girl and that life of the child was going to be extremely distressful. Her mother would shudder on hearing such words about her daughter. At that very time, Annie Sullivan entered their lives like a cool breeze. For many weeks, Annie tried to help Helen write by holding her tender hands in her own hands but she could not animate Helen's sensibility, consciousness and intelligence. Then, on 5 April, a miraculous incident took place in the life of Helen Keller. Helen remembered that incident clearly even after 60 years as she has provided a graphic account of her experience in her writing something like this:

As a teacher to Helen, Annie Sullivan had thoroughly devoted major part of her life to teach and train her. When Helen was sensible enough to find herself ready to go to college for study, she expressed her desire for the same to Annie. On hearing her wish, Annie felt like fresh shoots of Helen's growth germinating in her heart.

This happened near a well where I was standing with a mug in my hand. Annie was filling the same with water and as the water was touching my hand, she was using her fingers to write the word 'wa..t..er' on my other hand. I immediately understood the same. I felt some movement in the threads of sensibility and some sensation in my brain. This was the first joy of my life. I caught hold of Annie's hand out of excitement and requested her to teach me more new words that might be connected with the things I could touch. The sparks of words and their meanings kept flowing from one hand to the other and I developed the capacity to interpret words. That day, two delighted souls returned from that well - they were addressing each other as Helen and 'Teacher'.

As a teacher to Helen, Annie Sullivan had thoroughly devoted major part of her life to teach and train her. When Helen was sensible enough to find herself ready to go to college for study, she expressed her desire for the same to Annie. On hearing her wish, Annie felt like fresh shoots of Helen's growth germinating in her heart. She would sit with Helen in every class and keep on writing the lectures on her hand. She would burn the midnight oil to make Helen understand the books that were not available in braille. By now, Annie Sullivan had realised that Helen, despite being blind and deaf, was extraordinarily talented. Helen always had the craving to learn something new.

By the time Helen was 10 years old, she acquired proficiency in English, Latin, Greek, French and German languages entirely on account of her own hard work and unflinching support of Annie. The level of her intelligence grew to be even higher than that of her teacher.

However, the world fame that Helen had earned made Annie happier than Helen herself, as Annie was her true friend. She was such a friend that wanted to see the life of Helen at the pinnacle of success. And she devoted her entire life to help Helen reach that pinnacle. Today, the world remembers Annie and Helen not only as a teacher and a student but also as true friends who, despite being unrelated to each other, presented an extraordinary example of friendship to the world.

- **Respect Your Friends in Every Situation**: The key to a true friendship is mutual respect in every situation. Chanakya asserts, "Irrespective of whether a friend is wealthy or not, he should be always helped when in need even if that does not serve any self-interest." A friendship even with a trace of self-interest is not a true friendship. A friendship developed in the guise of deceit and treachery does not survive long. It is essential to be sincere in friendship. Chanakya maintains that it is better to remain friendless than having a friend who is treacherous, wicked and not trustworthy.

Rules of Friendship

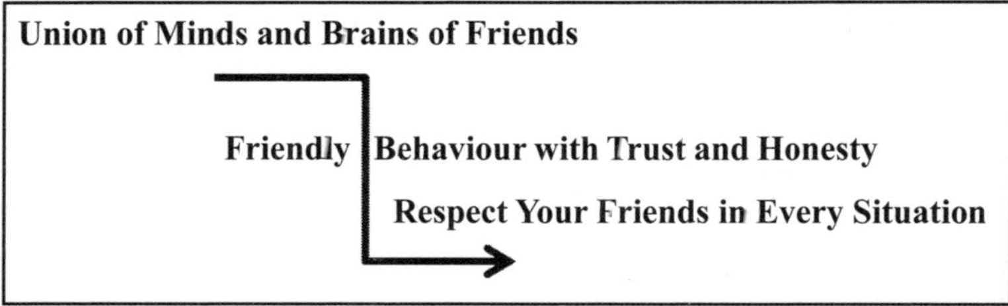

Today, everybody wants to improve his life. People take help from others for their own interests. Many people, out of their selfishness, just use pretension of friendship to get their work done and then never look back. Chanakya suggests that you should assess a person before making friends with him. Only the one who always wishes happiness and good health for his friend is a true friend.

Who is a friend?

Today, everybody wants to improve his life. People take help from others for their own interests. Many people, out of their selfishness, just use pretension of friendship to get their work done and then never look back. Chanakya suggests that you should assess a person before making friends with him. Only the one who always wishes happiness and good health for his friend is a true friend. He trusts his friend. Even when everybody else parts with a person in a worse situation, his true friend continues to stand by him. A sincere friend compliments in public and criticises in private.

Beware of Friendship with These People

Whereas Chanakya defines a true friend as the one who is always with his friend in his happiness and distress, he also does not forget to suggest, based on his experiences in life, that everybody should make friends only after due consideration and avoid making friends with persons having following characteristics:

- Getting angry even on trivial matters
- Having fickle mind and unreliable nature
- Complimenting in front and criticising on the back
- Mean in nature
- Treacherous, wicked and not trustworthy
- Deceitful and betrayer
- Having no respect for elders and the old.

Forms of Friendship

Human life is believed to be the best among 8.4 million different forms of life, as only a human has the ability to think and understand. A human being, on the strength of his intelligence, may make an impossible task possible and turn an adversity into congeniality and even use his brain to do something good for the entire world through his innovations. Being a social animal, it is impossible for a man to live alone.

Centuries ago, Chanakya had defined many forms of friends and had explained that not only a human being but even objects and other living beings could be friends of a person in different circumstances.

- **Medicine as friend to a diseased person**: For a person who is sick with disease and distraught with pain, medicine is the true friend for him. His pain cannot be treated without medicine. Even a true friend is helpless in such a situation. At the time of sickness, medicine is the only true and sincere friend for any person. He may get rid of the disease only after using the same.
- **Wealth also a friend in old age**: A person has to suffer maximum misery in his old age. In current times, children, after entering adulthood, get busy with their own affairs of livelihood. Hence, aged parents have often to go through a lot of hardships. They try to provide all kinds of comfort to their children hoping that their children would support them in old age, but those children get lost in their own world. Under such circumstance, money is the only friend and support for them in their old age. An aged person may get many of his desires satisfied with the help of money.
- **Books as friends**: Chanakya considers books also as good and true friends. He says, "Knowledge is just the Kamadhenu Cow capable of fulfilling all desires." Hence, students should read books. Not only students, even common people should inculcate the habit of reading books on regular basis. The finest books are the best friends. He, who makes friends with books, always attains progress in his life and keeps on marching ahead even in adverse circumstances.
- **Animals as friends**: Human life is believed to be the best among 8.4 million different forms of life, as only a human has the ability to think and understand. A human being, on the strength of his intelligence, may make an impossible task possible and turn an adversity into congeniality and even use

his brain to do something good for the entire world through his innovations. Being a social animal, it is impossible for a man to live alone. Some people are so much hurt in their lives by negative behaviour of others that they are just not ready to have faith in humans. Some people get so stressed by such negative behaviours and vitriolic outbursts of others in society that they even go to the extent of taking their own lives. They feel that it's not possible to lead this life alone and also it's not possible to make friends with other people. In such a case, they have one more option. Why only humans, even animals may be great friends. Books, wealth and medicines do not have feelings but animals have feelings, tears and even power to think. Cow, buffalo, dog, horse and donkey are the ones among animals who generally prove not only to be good friends but also trustworthy companions. Literature has plenty of such stories that have animals demonstrating exemplary forms of friendship. Even in wars, the horses of Rani Lakshmibai and Maharana Pratap have set outstanding examples of friendship.

Man may choose the form of friendship as per his convenience. He may then go ahead with the same and attain success in life.

Forms of Friendship

Lessons from Acharya

Man is a social animal. Hence, people should help their friends. Friendship should be unbiased and free from deceit and treachery. Friends even play an important role in making a nation powerful. A powerful ruler should support weaker rulers with complete sincerity and devotion; that would ensure for him support from them with equally sincere devotion in times of adverse circumstances. A trustworthy person only can be a suitable and great friend. Even a friendship, though not involving any relationship, may set such standards that may be remembered for centuries.

❑

Lessons from Guru

Acharya's Pearls of Wisdom

- *Debt of a guru can't be paid back even with the most valuable object in this world.*
- *Man develops cognition of the Supreme Power and understanding of the mysteries and philosophy of soul and the Supreme Spirit only through a guru.*
- *It's not possible to acquire knowledge without a guru.*

Who is a Guru?

Guru is knowledge. A guru is the one who imparts knowledge. Mainly, teacher, acharya, kulguru and diksha guru are the people who impart knowledge. India has a long history of gurus with Gautam Buddha, Ramakrishna Paramahansa, Nanak Dev, Maharshi Ramana, Swami Samarth, Swami Vivekananda and

Chanakya being the most prominent examples. Great poet Kabir had also accorded importance to a guru through one of his couplets as below.

गुरु गोबिंद दोऊ खड़े, काके लागूँ पाय।
बलिहारी गुरु आपने जिन गोबिंद दियो बताय।

It means that if teacher and God are both standing in front, one should bow his head to the teacher, as it's the teacher who imparts knowledge about God as well as everything else. A good and ideal guru always envisages progress for his disciple. He develops his disciple's strengths to make him capable of earning name, fame and wealth. Not only that, a real guru goes and finds out a worthy disciple and then infuses morals and values into him. Though Krishna was just a charioteer for Arjuna in the Mahabharata war, he imparted knowledge to Arjuna as a guru when the latter got emotional. That very knowledge is known as the gist of the Gita. Whenever a guru like Krishna enters the life of a person, his life gets filled with morality, virtuousness, knowledge and pragmatism, and immorality and depravity are completely eliminated.

Guru Chanakya Eliminated Immorality and Depravity

For uprooting Dhanananda, it was necessary to install a worthy and righteous ruler in his place. Chanakya started looking for a suitable candidate for the same. One day, he was just passing through a ground where some children were playing a game of a king and his ministers. He looked at the boy who was acting as the king. He was quite impressed by the fearlessness, brilliance and leadership qualities of the boy and he got an inkling that he had found the future emperor of Magadha.

During the period of Chanakya, Magadha was the largest state in India. Dhanananda, the 9th king of Nanda dynasty, was its ruler at that time. He always indulged in luxuries and was a tyrannical and extremely selfish ruler. His ministers kept on reminding him about the welfare of his state but he would always rebuke and send them back and revert to his indulgences. One day, during a philosophical discourse, Dhanananda misbehaved with the scholars very badly. When Chanakya tried to convey the truth in hard-hitting words instead of indulging in sycophancy towards Dhanananda, he fumed and got Chanakya evicted from his durbar. This insult hurt Chanakya badly and he took a vow not to tie his tuft of hair until he uprooted Dhanananda completely. For uprooting Dhanananda, it was necessary to install a worthy and righteous ruler in his place. Chanakya started looking for a suitable candidate for the same. One day, he was just passing through an open ground where some children were playing a game of a king and his ministers. He looked at the boy who was acting as the king. He was quite impressed by the fearlessness, brilliance and leadership qualities of the boy and he got an inkling that he had found the future emperor of Magadha. This way, an ideal guru got his worthy disciple. All the events that took place later leading to the making of Magadha Emperor Chandragupta are parts of history now. Chanakya had made Chandragupta Maurya adept both at statecraft and martial arts.

24 Gurus of Saint Dattatreya

He who imparts knowledge irrespective of the form or place is a guru. Saint Dattatreya gained experience of this living world very minutely and in the process, accepted discipleship of 24 gurus. These 24 gurus are as following:

1. Earth
2. Wind
3. Sky
4. Water
5. Yama
6. Fire

7. Moon
8. Sun
9. Pigeon
10. Python
11. Ocean
12. Moth
13. Honeybee
14. Bumblebee
15. Elephant
16. Deer, Fish
17. Courtesan
18. Crow
19. Innocent child
20. Woman husking rice
21. Blacksmith
22. Serpent
23. Spider
24. Wasp

Before accepting discipleship of all the above gurus, Saint Dattatreya had undertaken detailed observation and examined their activities very minutely and then only had made the conclusion that any person who took lessons from the above 24 gurus would be able to make his life meaningful.

1. **Earth**: Dattatreya treated the earth as his first guru, as the earth patiently bears everything right from sun, cold, rains and treads and never gets angry.
2. **Wind**: Perpetually moving and carrying fragrance but not being the fragrance itself, thus exhibiting complete

detachment, wind teaches us to always remain dynamic in this life.

3. **Sky**: Despite being magnificent and limitless, the sky is never proud of itself. This very quality of the sky fascinated Saint Dattatreya.
4. **Water**: This ordinary-looking fluid supports all kinds of life. This greatness adorns a guru.
5. **Yama:** Yama, who, keeping control on accretion, provides relaxation to those exhausted from fatigue, is also a guru.
6. **Fire**: Saint Dattatreya has also accepted discipleship of fire that is eternally brilliant and that affects all.
7. **Moon**: The moon seems to wax and wane but it never gets disheartened and holds its spirit to move ahead. This is the greatness of a guru.
8. **Sun**: The Sun's attribute of illuminating everything in this nature from its own brilliance is the quality of a guru only. A guru, being himself illuminated, illuminates the true nature of all things to his disciples and makes them enlightened. Hence, the Sun also is a guru.
9. **Pigeon**: A pigeon gets caught in a snare because of his greed for grains and then loses his life. It thus cautions others that greed is a great curse that takes anybody to downfall. Hence, it is also a guru.
10. **Python**: During cold season, the body of the python goes into spasm and it is unable to move out much. It hence devours whatever creature it comes across and even survives by eating soil only. Because of its endurance, it is also a worthy guru.
11. **Ocean**: Ocean that provides pure water to clouds even though its own water is saline is also a guru.
12. **Moth**: The moth risks his life for attaining its goal. This very devotion of the moth makes one accept its discipleship.

13. **Honeybee**: A honeybee steadfastly collects honey and then gives that over to others, thus conveying the message that a person should be altruistic and not selfish. Thus, a honeybee is also a guru.
14. **Bumblebee**: A bumblebee loses its life because of its obsession. Hence, he is worthy to be a guru.
15. **Elephant**: A lustful elephant gets trapped easily. This conveys that one should be always beware of the fetters of infatuation. Thus, the elephant teaching this lesson is also a guru.
16. Deer, Fish: Observing a deer getting caught by a hunter and a fish agonising in the net because of its craving for delicious food, it may be learnt that greed can even take one's life.
17. **Courtesan**: Pingala, the courtesan, giving a message of caution even when she was filled with remorse, is also worthy to be respected as a guru.
18. **Crow**: The crow's policy of cunningness and selfishness eventually leads to detrimental results. Hence, one should treat it also a guru and remain cautious.
19. **Innocent Child**: An innocent child remains immersed in his own world away from hatred, worries, disputes, greed, etc. Hence, man should also try to be like that.
20. **Woman Husking Rice**: A woman husking rice is able to skilfully manage multiple tasks at the same time. Hence, she is also equivalent to a guru.

The above 24 gurus of Saint Dattatreya are unique because of their specific characteristics and that is the reason that Dattatreya has accepted their discipleship. Any prudent person who keeps following the above gurus becomes extremely sagacious and knowledgeable and leads a successful life. Nobody can attain knowledge without a guru. Man may, depending on his own ideology and nature even add new gurus.

21. **Blacksmith**: The way a blacksmith heats an iron piece in a forge and shapes the same teaches us the lesson that if a person burns himself repeatedly, he creates a new identity for himself after depuration.

22. **Serpent**: A serpent gets sad himself after afflicting others. This shows that it is stubborn and short tempered.

23. **Spider**: Just as a spider weaves its web but never gets caught itself in the same, every person also creates his world around himself as per his feelings.

24. **Wasp**: A wasp catches an insect and, getting impressed by its buzzing, allows that insect to grow into a wasp. This shows that any kind of transmogrification is possible with the help of assiduity and concentration.

The above 24 gurus of Saint Dattatreya are unique because of their specific characteristics and that is the reason that Dattatreya has accorded them the status of a guru. Any prudent person who keeps following the above gurus becomes extremely sagacious and knowledgeable and leads a successful life. Nobody can attain knowledge without a guru. Man may, depending on his own ideology and nature, even add new gurus.

These new gurus may include a friend, a book, any bird or animal, any plant or tree or anything else. True friends and good books generally prove to be great gurus. With regard to books, there is even a saying that good books should bear a label like "this book may change your life". Gurus are like that only; they transform their disciples by developing their qualities and endow them affluence and fame in abundance.

Greatest Gurus and Disciples of the World

1. **Rishi Sandipani - Krishna**: Rishi Sandipani made Krishna a yugpurush by imparting him the knowledge of Vedas and

Upanishads. Shri Krishna had learnt 64 art forms in 64 days at Rishi Sandipani's ashram in Ujjain.

2. **Chanakya - Chandragupta:** Chanakya installed his disciple Chandragupta as a great emperor of India and established a united India.

3. **Dronacharya - Arjuna**: Dronacharya was royal perceptor to both the Pandavas and Kauravas. He was instrumental in making Arjuna the greatest archer on the earth. To continue that legacy, the Government of India has instituted 'Dronacharya Award' and 'Arjuna Award'. These awards are presented to deserving gurus and disciples respectively.

4. **Aristotle - Alexander**: The great philosopher Aristotle was the guru of Alexander. He had extensive knowledge of philosophy, politics, poetry, ethics, astrology and medicine. Because of his guru, Alexander is still considered immortal in the world history.

5. **Henry Murray - Newton:** Newton was quite weak both physically and mentally in his childhood. In the situation, it was Henry Murray, a teacher in philosophy, who helped him regain his self-confidence and enthusiasm. As a result, Newton was able to undertake great discoveries for the world.

6. **Ramdas Samarth - Shivaji:** Swami Ramdas was a saint. He chose the energetic warrior Shivaji to help the people get rid of tyrannical rulers of that time. Shivaji made guru Ramdas immortal and it was because of his guidance only that Shivaji rose from a commander to 'Chhatrapati Shivaji'.

7. **Neem Karoli Baba - Mark Zuckerberg:** Mark Zuckerberg, the founder of Facebook, was once feeling very disturbed. The founder of Apple, Steve Jobs suggested him to visit Baba Neem Karoli at Kainchi Dham located in Nainital in India in order to attain peace. Mark did feel a fresh energy and sense of peace after visiting the place.

8. **Ramakrishna Paramahansa - Swami Vivekananda:** It was in the company of Ramakrishna Paramahansa that Swami Vivekananda established the spiritual supremacy of India in the entire world. Only after that, India was given the title of 'Vishwa Guru'.

9. **Mother - Child:** In the entire world, a mother is the first guru of her child. That's why mother has been placed equivalent to God. A mother ensures all-round development of her child. Everybody is aware of the life of Thomas Alva Edison and how his mother helped him get rid of his intellectual weakness and raised him to become the greatest inventor of the world. The schools had expelled Edison accusing him to be addlebrained. In that situation, his mother not only took the role of his guru but also developed his self-confidence and knowledge to the extent that he grew to be known as the Father of Great Inventions.

10. **Teacher - Student:** Only a teacher imparts knowledge, advice and guidance to a student. Dr. Sarvepalli Radhakrishnan was himself a teacher. He desired his birthday 5 September to be dedicated to all teachers and since then, this day is being celebrated as 'Teachers' Day'.

Why is a Guru Necessary in Life?

A guru is required in the life of a person to make him aware of the sense of right and wrong. Age is no bar to be a guru. Many a time, a young person, on account of his talent and ability, goes on to become guru of a person much older than him.

A guru is required in the life of a person to make him aware of the sense of right and wrong. Age is no bar to be a guru. Many a time, a young person, on account of his talent and ability, goes on to become guru of a person much older than him. Jahnvi and Amar Satvik of Haryana are examples of the same. Jahnvi is an inspirational orator. Amar Satvik provides online help to lakhs of aspirants preparing for IAS examination. He is hardly 14 years old at the moment. Born in Telangana, Amar had started his web channel at the age of 10 years itself. The number of subscribers to his channel exceeds 2.33 lakhs. Despite both being students themselves, they are gurus and ideals for lakhs of people.

Gu + Ru

In a way, the word GURU may be interpreted as Gu + Ru = **Gu**n (Qualities) + **Ru**paya (Money).

Guru is the one who develops good qualities of his disciple in the way that he becomes capable of earning wealth through hard-work and ethical means and enjoys the pleasures of life. Only an able guru can have the courage to transform a human being into a man and then into a great man. It's essential for a guru also to be worthy. If any thing or living being with negativity is accepted as guru, it should always be based on some positive and meaningful purpose just as Saint Dattatreya had embraced positive messages even from negative attributes.

A guru like Chanakya will be remembered for centuries for creating a great emperor like Chandragupta.

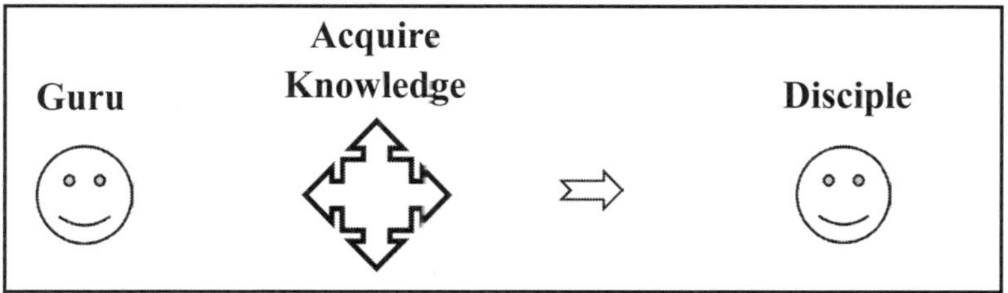

Lessons from Chanakya

When an ideal guru and an ideal disciple come together, it results in a miracle and tyranny and atrocities give way to fresh rule and great endeavours. It's the duty of a guru to impart all the knowledge relating to various strategies to his disciple without being worried about his own life. At the same time, it's also the duty of a disciple to follow all the instructions of his guru. He should give due respect to all people and creatures contemporary to his guru and try to learn from them and make his life positive and successful.

❑

A Wicked Person

Acharya's Pearls of Wisdom

- *Wicked persons are like thorns; hence, either rub them down with your shoes or change your path to avoid them.*
- *Wicked persons have the flair to be jealous of the progress of others.*
- *A serpent has its poison in its teeth, a bee has the same in its head and a scorpion has its poison in its tail but a wicked personhas his entire body poisonous.*

Who is a Wicked Person?

A human being is the one that has shortcomings and that makes mistakes. Despite his shortcomings and mistakes, he does not forget his humanity. Humanity means respecting humanness in spite of all shortcomings. There are two kinds of humans - virtuous and wicked. A virtuous person primarily possesses positive feelings. They tread their own path and are always prepared to help others. On the contrary, wicked people are selfish, jealous and greedy. They always have negative ideas. They never feel good to see the progress of others or progress of the country. At every step, they consider only themselves to be the best. A wicked person leads others to downfall. Hence, it is wise to avoid such people. There is a couplet like this:

क्वचित् सर्पेपि मित्रत्वमियात् नैव खलः क्वचित्।
न शेषशायिनीऽप्यस्य वशे दुर्योधनः हरेः।।

In other words, even a serpent may be befriended but a wicked person can never be made friends with. Even Duryodhan could not become a friend of Lord Vishnu sleeping on Sheshnag.

How to Recognise a Wicked Person?

Wicked people, many a time, try to hide their normal behaviour to accomplish their objectives. Chanakya advises that a simple and gentle person should have the disposition to recognise wicked people. In order to identify a wicked person, Chanakya suggests keeping a watch on his conduct:

- He who is always angry and keeps on secreting venom through his words is a wicked person.
- People inflicting harm on their friends and relatives and keeping company with depraved persons are also wicked.
- One should beware of a person with mysterious behaviour. Such a person generally has wicked nature.
- People who do not shy away from indulging in any nefarious activities to acquire wealth are wicked.

Recognise people with such nature and try to stay away from them.

Why Are Some People Wicked?

Chanakya has considered wicked people even more dangerous than venomous snakes and poisonous plants. He also believes that mostly people devoid of moral values are wicked. Those very people who do not possess self-confidence, wisdom, assiduity and honesty indulge in unethical deeds. Mostly, the vicious nature of a person has its roots in his family and the environment in which he grew. Hence, parents should try to provide a safe and decent environment to their children. A child learns by observing his parents and people around him. If parents demonstrate virtuous behaviour, their children would also imbibe those virtues since his childhood itself. In addition to that, it is important for the children to get decent environment and good company when they are growing up. It's the company that shapes our words and deeds. Chanakya has clarified that even innocents get punished just like wicked people because of their company. Just as even wet sticks get burnt when placed on fire along with dry sticks, innocent people also may have to suffer loss of life and property because of their being in company of wicked people.

Chanakya has considered wicked people even more dangerous than venomous snakes and poisonous plants. He also believes that mostly people devoid of moral values are wicked. Only such people who do not possess self-confidence, wisdom, assiduity and honesty indulge in unethical deeds.

Wicked people remain untouched by virtues like self-consciousness, tolerance, righteousness, simplicity and determination. They do not hesitate in indulging in even the most nefarious activities. The perversions exist in our society because of these wicked people only. Hence, in order to prevent development of evil character, students in schools should be imparted such practical education that is capable of stopping them from indulging in nefarious deeds even under the most trying situations of their lives. A person with knowledge and wisdom knows how to come out victorious in any situation. Hence, education system should be suitably fine-tuned to ensure that children in a society grow to become only righteous and noble individuals.

Stay Away from Wicked People

Chanakya had studied at Taxila. Taxila was an important centre for education in ancient India. Students from entire country and abroad used to study there. Personalities of the students studying at Taxila used to shine bright like a diamond. The curriculum there included important subjects like jurisprudence, politics, medicine, social welfare and national security besides Vedas, archery, eighteen art forms and controlling elephants and horses. The brilliant mind of Chanakya had understood this at a very early age itself that wicked people were like thorns and they needed to be either crushed completely or avoided entirely, as any encounter with such people resulted in damages only.

One day, while going along a pathway, Chanakya stepped on a thorny shrub known as Kusha. The thorns in the shrub inflicted a big wound on Chanakya's feet. Seeing that, he took a vow to uproot the thorny shrub completely. He immediately came back with some buttermilk and a spade and started hitting the shrub badly. After a lot of effort, he finally succeeded in uprooting the shrub. He then said, "A wicked person and a poisonous shrub must be uprooted and destroyed immediately, else they inflict even more damages once they grow up."

Chanakya spared no effort for attaining his goal. He dedicated his entire life for the country. Eventually, his vow was fulfilled and he was successful in removing Dhanananda and installing an able ruler Chandragupta Maurya in his place. Chandragupta was a disciple of Chanakya only.

King Dhanananda of Pataliputra was also a wicked person. He never bothered for security of the state or welfare of his subjects. Chanakya, after reaching Pataliputra, cautioned Dhanananda and suggested that he should try to eliminate all hostilities among various smaller states of the country and bind them all together in one thread. Not only that, he also advised him to stay away from wine and other worldly indulgences and to focus on the welfare of his subjects. Chanakya's acerbic words left Dhanananda fuming with anger. He rudely insulted Chanakya in his open court. Chanakya then took a vow not to tie his tuft of hair until he uprooted wicked Dhanananda completely. And Chanakya spared no effort for attaining his goal. He dedicated his entire life for the country. Eventually, his vow was fulfilled and he was successful in removing Dhanananda and installing an able ruler Chandragupta Maurya in his place. Chandragupta was a disciple of Chanakya only. Chanakya had decided to make him ruler after noticing his merits in his childhood itself.

This way, Chanakya demonstrated, as a lesson in the ethics of life, that despite receiving all the goodness from others, wicked persons, like venomous animals, never give up their immorality.

Evil Person

Mythological scriptures have umpteen examples where wicked people persisted with their immoral character and evil deeds despite being treated gentlemanly by others.

Most significant examples of such characters are Kansa, Duryodhana, Hiranyakashyap, Jarasandha and Shishupal. They received humane treatment multiple times but they did not give up their evil character. Krishna even pardoned Shishupal for his 100 sins but Shishupal still did not mend his ways. An evil person is cruel by nature. For him, words like sympathy, affection and love have no meaning. They even do not give any importance to relationships. Family, society and country have no significance for wicked people. The only aim such people have is to fulfil their self-interest. Their immoral and sinful attitude does not diminish even when they grow older. Such people do not miss any chance to mistreat simple, ascetic and prudent persons. Such people inflict injuries on an ascetic, patient and prudent person when he is busy with his own jobs shutting his eyes to their intentions.

Gentleman - He is brimming with moral values. Such a person is very significant for development of a country.

Wicked Person - He leads to destruction. He does not have moral values.

Wicked people lack in moral values. They are just self-centred. They do not possess self-confidence, knowledge, concentration and honesty. It's difficult for a person to earn anything in his life in the absence of skills.

Lessons from Chanakya

Wicked people lack in moral values. They are just self-centred. They do not possess self-confidence, knowledge, concentration and honesty. It's difficult for a person to earn anything in his life in the absence of skills. Hence, they turn rogue and evil. They try to acquire everything through theft or other unethical means and try to harm anybody they encounter. It is better to stay away from evil people, as noble persons have to face a lot of hardships and difficulties only because of such people. Company of such people gives rise to depravity and vices only.

❑

Kinds of Sick Persons

Acharya's Pearls of Wisdom

- *Greed is the greatest malady.*
- *He who is afflicted by envy and hatred for wealth, beauty, heroism, decent parentage, prosperity, good fortune and fame of others is incurable. He can never be treated for this affliction.*
- *Bad-mouthing is a serious malady. Beware of the same.*

The Sick and The Sickness

Sickness refers to a malady or disease and sick means a person afflicted by any kind of malady. Change in composition of any part of the body or weakening in its ability to function normally is called sickness. Sickness slowly leads a person to death. Life is quite precious. Once afflicted by a malady, this starts falling apart.

A sick person is not able to attend to his duties properly. He is not able to even live his life to the fullest. He remains unwell.

There are nine basic emotions in a human being. These are - Love, Humour, Anger, Sorrow, Courage, Disgust, Fear, Surprise and Peace. These are the emotions that induce feelings in response to external situations. A person gets realisation of love, compassion, jealousy or courage through these emotions only. Existence of Navarasa is essential in life.

Kinds of Sickness

Sickness is mainly of two kinds - physical and mental. There may be many reasons for a physical sickness like bacteria, virus or microplasma. There are many infectious diseases also like T.B., cough and cold that may get transmitted from one person to another person quite easily.

Mental sickness is related primarily to maladies of mind. The sick person remains healthy physically but his conduct and behaviour undergo severe changes. Many mental maladies are more dangerous than physical maladies. Besides physical and mental sickness, are you aware of other maladies that may be equally harmful for people?

How Navarasas Turn into Disease?

Navarasa also may turn into maladies. You find this a bit strange but this is true. These are the maladies that are not accepted as maladies by people. And they themselves fail to even sense when they get afflicted with such maladies because of overabundance of these Navarasa.

Navarasas

There are nine basic emotions in a human being. These are - Love, Humour, Anger, Sorrow, Courage, Disgust, Fear, Surprise and

Peace. These are the emotions that induce feelings in response to external situations. A person gets realisation of love, compassion, jealousy or courage through these very emotions. Existence of Navarasas is essential in life. Pundit Ramchandra Shukla, a professor in Hindi literature, had said, "It's not enjoyable to always eat sweet food only; even sour and spicy food once in a while appears delicious." This means that there should be a balance among all the nine emotions in life. Too much of sweet food or too much of sour food makes a person sick very soon. Similarly, when some of the emotions of Navarasas develop much more than others, they take the form of maladies. Love, anger, sorrow, fear and disgust are significant ones among them.

Forms of Navarasas

- **Love**

Love here refers to lust or sexual desire. Chanakya considers lust the most powerful enemy of man in his life. He has treated this as equivalent to an incurable disease, a disease that can't be treated by any medicine. A too lusty person is destined to his doom. Growing atrocities against women give rise to immoral activities in the society and the country. The malady of lust can be cured only with knowledge.

Sorrow wears down a person just like termites. Tragedies like sudden demise of near and dear ones and heavy loss in business jolt a person badly. The shock is sometimes so lethal that it even takes away the life of the impacted person.

- **Anger**

Anger is a very prominent emotion. It exists in every living being on this earth. Just as even a delicious meal becomes poison for our body if taken in excess, too much of anger ruins and depraves a person.

- **Sorrow**

Sorrow wears down a person just like termites. Tragedies like sudden demise of near and dear ones and heavy loss in business jolt a person badly. The shock is sometimes so lethal that it even takes away the life of the impacted person. This emotion hence should be there in a reasonable measure only. If this goes out of balance, that is to say, if the person after getting distressed goes into a state of inconsolable melancholy, the entire family along with him has to face a lot of difficulties. Chanakya maintains that grieving turns the body of a person into a dwelling place for maladies. This only results in suffering for the body of that person and happiness for his enemies.

- **Fear**

Fear is very powerful among the Navarasas. This places constraints on a person, restrains him and develops feelings of anxiety and worry in him. This anxiety and worry spoil everything and the person almost loses his reasoning power. Fear wears down the energy and vitality of the person. Chanakya has considered fear to be extremely lethal for a human life. Psychologists link fear to cognitive distortion. This is essentially centred in the brain of a person. A severely frightened person is able to neither live his life to the fullest nor use his intelligence to give proper direction to his endeavours. Fear wears down the entire inner strength of the person. There is only one effective method to overcome fear and that is to face the fear and do the same things that made you feel afraid. If a person is afraid of darkness, he should try to calmly stay in darkness. Once he overcomes his fear of darkness, none of the fears would be able to overwhelm him. For a person who knows how to overcome a fear, it becomes easy to face any kind of fear. Fear is also a malady. Chanakya advises that the best way for a person to get rid of this malady is to keep moving ahead towards his desired goals with sincere and positive frame of mind. It is not easy to frighten a person who is focussed on his intended goals.

Chanakya advises that the best way for a person to get rid of this malady is to keep moving ahead towards his desired goals with sincere and positive frame of mind. It is not easy to frighten a person who is focussed on his intended goals.

- **Disgust**

A feeling of revulsion against filth and immoral activities is beneficial but if the situation is just the opposite meaning that if a person starts feeling disgusted to see other healthy and well-to-do people, he is certainly doomed.

This emotion even awakens other emotions, primarily jealousy, greed and slander already present in a person.

- **Envy**

Slander is also a serious malady. Chanakya considers this to be a ***'maharog'****. A person inflicted with this disease does not have even an inkling of the fact that he is wasting his precious time and effort on slandering somebody. One who stands away from slander keeps moving ahead on his path; such people are generally brilliant and intellectuals. Those who fall in its clutches remain inflicted with the malady of slander for life.*

In colloquial terms, envy is also called 'जलन' (Jalan). 'जलन' means 'जलना' (Burning). Envy is an incurable disease such that its flames burn the very person who is consumed with it. Many a time, the person who is being envied is himself not aware of the fact that somebody is burning in the flames of envy towards him. Chanakya considers people envying the prosperity of others as incurable patients. Such people think that they are targeting others but in fact they themselves become targets of such envy. Envy can never help anybody prosper. Only people who move ahead with positive attitude see their mind, brain and opinions flourish. When a person allows envy to grow, he gets only hate and revenge in return. An envious person gets enraged on finding somebody being admired. The burden of envy is quite heavy. A person can't take long steps with that burden on his shoulders. Hence, one should abstain from burdening himself with envy. There is no place for envy in the life of a person who treads his path with sincerity and positive attitude. In fact, he does not have the time for wasting on worthless emotions like envy.

- **Slander**

Satirist Harishankar Parsai has mentioned in his essay 'Ninda Ras' that 'Slander germinates out of inferiority complex and weakness'. People having weakness and inferiority complex only indulge in slander. Slander means making false statements damaging to others' reputation. A person gets a lot of pleasure and peace in slandering somebody but when he himself becomes an object of slander, he finds himself in the midst of a storm. He feels like scratching the face of that person slandering him and teaching him a lesson such that the person will never again indulge in slandering anybody. Slander is also a serious malady. Chanakya considers this to be a 'maharog'. A person inflicted with this disease does not have even an inkling of the fact that he is wasting his precious time and effort on slandering somebody. One who stands away from slander keeps moving ahead on his path; such people are generally brilliant and intellectuals. Those who fall in its clutches remain inflicted with the malady of slander for life.

- **Greed**

Chanakya asserts that greed is like a mirage that never dies down. This always keeps the person agitated. He is always under unending craving because of his discontentment and dissatisfaction. His abdominal hunger may be satisfied with food but the hunger of greed does not get satisfied till his last breath. Even on his death-bed, he keeps on thinking like 'If only this had happened! If only that had happened!' A person who learns to be sincerely content with whatever little he has never finds himself short of prosperity and happiness. A greedy person can never be happy and prosperous.

Just as a diseased person does not feel fit and healthy, a person afflicted with maladies like excess of love, sorrow, fear, anger, disgust, envy, slander and greed also does not feel to be all right. Envy, slander and greed are such maladies that cripple a person badly. Hence, one should stay away from them and move ahead with his endeavours with positive thinking.

Kinds of Sick Persons

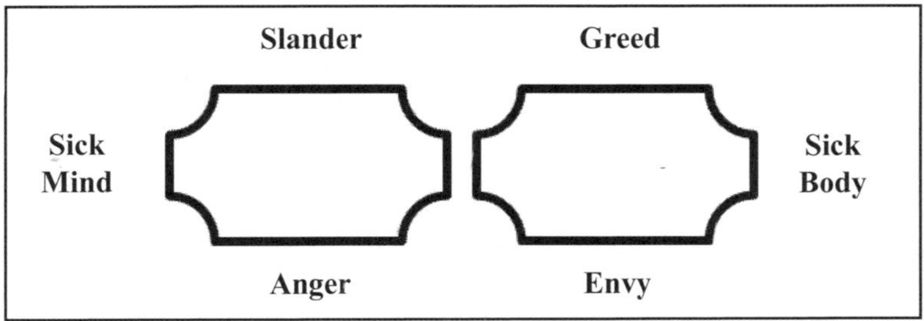

Balance Among Navarasas

Existence of the nine emotions (Navarasas) is essential for every person. A person devoid of these emotions is not called normal. The emotions should exist in a person in well-balanced quantities. Negative emotions like envy and anger should be utilised in a positive way. A person may strike a balance with practice and live his life to the fullest. Everything is possible if there is desire and enthusiasm in one's mind.

Lessons from Chanakya

Emotions like greed, slander, envy, lust, sorrow, fear, anger and disgust ruin a person. These maladies are worse than physical maladies. Physical maladies can be cured anyway with medicines but maladies like greed, envy and anger shatter a person both physically and mentally. And it's all the more surprising that people do not accept them as maladies at all. A person gets afflicted with many diseases because of these emotions and he still feels that there are other reasons for his sickness. There is only one way to keep away from them - positive knowledge and positive thoughts.

❑

Moral Politics

Acharya's Pearls of Wisdom

- *Money acquired through sinful and immoral acts stays hardly for ten years. Entire money along with interest vanishes in the eleventh year.*
- *Just as the new moon is worshipped instead of the full moon, even a poor and low-born person having moral values is worthy of reverence and adoration.*
- *Just as sandalwood does not get poisonous despite its tree being entwined by venomous snakes and just as a flower grown on soil does not get drenched in the smell of the soil, a noble person does not fail to remember his nobility and virtues even in the company of wicked people.*

Chanakya, who gave a new identity to India and Pataliputra in the world, always led his life with simplicity and humble disposition. He could have acquired all the desirable luxuries just on a single command; instead, he created an exemplary precedent by his humble behaviour and simple life.

'Raj' and 'Niti' = 'Rajniti' (Politics)

'Rajneeti' combines the words 'Raj' and 'Neeti'. 'Raj' means 'to rule' and 'Niti' means tactics or common sense used to accomplish a task properly. *Nitishastra* is a treatise on the common sense required for a person to follow the path of righteousness. When 'Raj' is combined with the same, it becomes a system that guides a political power. In real sense, 'Rajniti' or politics is the system that helps uplift the social, economic and political status of common people.

Politics is a word that encompasses all the aspects of development for a country. A nation grows when everybody grows. When politics becomes a tool in the hands of a few powerful ruling elite, it leads the entire country and its people to downfall. Politics and corruption are inextricably linked. When there is a situation where members of a family or office or company indulge in disparaging each other, it is often remarked that growth of that family or office or company is getting hindered because of politics in the family or office or company. Only a moral and virtuous person can give a new direction to a country and its politics. People who only desire fulfilment of their self-interest have no concern for the growth of their country and its people. Common people, in such a case, struggle even for their basic needs and remote areas of the country do not see even a ray of development or facilities. Chanakya maintained that only a person who did not seek any self-interest and who was free from corrupt behaviour could create best strategies in politics. Chanakya, who gave a new identity to India and Pataliputra in the world, always led his life with simplicity and humble disposition. He could have acquired all the desirable luxuries just on a single command; instead, he created an exemplary precedent by his humble behaviour and simple life.

Mystery of Two Lamps

A businessman was quite impressed by Chanakya's honesty and the policies implemented by him. He wanted to meet him and invite him to his place. When he went to see him, Chanakya was busy scrutinising some official project. The businessman decided to wait there. He just had a look at Chanakya's hut. Finding the same to be so simple with signs of a humble life, he was quite surprised. He said to himself, "The guru and adviser who gave India such a great emperor lives such a simple life!" At that very moment, Chanakya happened to see the businessman. He said with all humility, "Please wait for some more time. I am just to finish my work."

The businessman went into deep thoughts to see his humility and concentration. A few moments later, he heard the voice, "Now please go ahead, I have finished my work."

The businessman just came out of his thoughts. He observed that Chanakya had put off a lamp and lit another lamp. He was perplexed. Anxious to understand the purpose of the same, he asked, "Guruji, the lamp was already burning. Then, why did you put off the same and light another lamp? What is the mystery of these two lamps?"

Chanakya replied with a smile, "Gentleman, I was working on an official task then and hence I was using the lamp with oil bought at state's cost. I am now using the lamp with oil bought at my personal cost as I am attending to a personal job. I keep the two accounts separate."

The businessman was surprised to hear that. He bowed to Chanakya and said, "The country that has virtuous personalities like you managing the affairs of state can never be stopped from marching ahead by even the greatest obstacles in this world."

Chanakya was a righteous person. He was great scholar and very knowledgeable. A knowledgeable person may attain anything like wealth, fame and authority on the strength of his knowledge and wisdom but when the same knowledge gets mixed with unscrupulousness and corruption, it creates havoc. The shine of honesty and self-confidence in the personality of a righteous person does not fade in any situation. An honest and righteous person is able to surmount any problem or adversity. Politics flourishes only when the same is nourished with the fertilisers of honesty, dedication and wisdom. Politics, in their absence, leads to anarchy and invites unwanted battles. Hence, any field, be it politics or any other one, essentially needs righteousness and righteous people. The foundations of honesty and unscrupulousness last for generations.

Impact of Honesty and Dishonesty on Children

Chanakya firmly believes that the merits and demerits of parents and their conduct definitely impact their children. If a person is dishonest, characterless and has wicked disposition, his children also possess the same vices. In today's busy era, people are often seen complaining that their children are disobedient or they keep lying or they indulge in violent acts etc. etc. Psychologists believe that children can't be made noble and open-hearted just by preaching them honesty and righteousness round-the-clock. Instead, they learn from the conduct of their parents. Children are the shadows of their parents. A shadow just follows its real object. Hence, instead of preaching children, parents should themselves try to tread the path that they want their children to follow.

If a person himself is dishonest and has wicked disposition, howsoever he may try to portray himself as a noble person, his children would definitely realise the truth from his expression and body language. Hence, in order to ensure that children grow to be noble and righteous persons, it is essential that parents also possess moral righteousness.

If a person himself is dishonest and has wicked disposition, howsoever he may try to portray himself as a noble person, his children would definitely realise the truth from his expression and body language. Hence, in order to ensure that children grow to be noble and righteous persons, it is essential that parents also possess moral righteousness.

Foundations of Childhood

Childhood is usually quite susceptive, tender and supple. It just flows in the direction where it finds a path. A 10-year-old girl Ayushi got her marks in Mathematics, Hindi and Social Sciences revised down not once but four times. Two times her teacher had made mistakes in addition of marks and other two times, wrong answers were marked correct. Once she got the answer sheets, Ayushi willingly got those unwitting mistakes corrected. The teacher asked her, "Beta, are you not sad to get your marks reduced?"

Acharya Chanakya has candidly put all his ideas on statecraft into words in his famous treatise ***Arthashastra****. He had then said, "For common good, I am presenting all those hidden mysteries of politics that, if imbibed, would make a person omniscient. Success would undoubtedly chase the person who follows the principles enumerated in this treatise."*

Ayushi then gave a very impressive and interesting reply. She said, "Madam, if my answer is wrong, I do not deserve marks for the same. I did not do anything great, I have just followed what my mother does."

The teacher was amazed to hear that. She had realised well that in order to impart good behaviour to children and provide them a suitable environment for growth, it was necessary for the parents themselves to be righteous and stay in a positive environment.

Moral Politics

Both the ruler and the subjects of a state are happy under moral politics. Only he who discharges his responsibilities towards his subjects capably is called a good politician and a good statesman. Chandragupta established a grand empire during his almost 24-year-long rule under the guidance of Chanakya and his brilliant statecraft. Acharya Chanakya has candidly put all his ideas on statecraft into words in his famous treatise *Arthashastra*. He had then said, "For common good, I am presenting all those hidden mysteries of politics that, if imbibed, would make a person omniscient. Success would undoubtedly chase the person who follows the principles enumerated in this treatise."

It is sad that politics of today abounds only in anarchy and allegations and counter-allegations on opponents and it has lost its primary context. If politics today were based on the morals propounded by Chanakya, everybody would get equal rights and prosperity and happiness would be there everywhere.

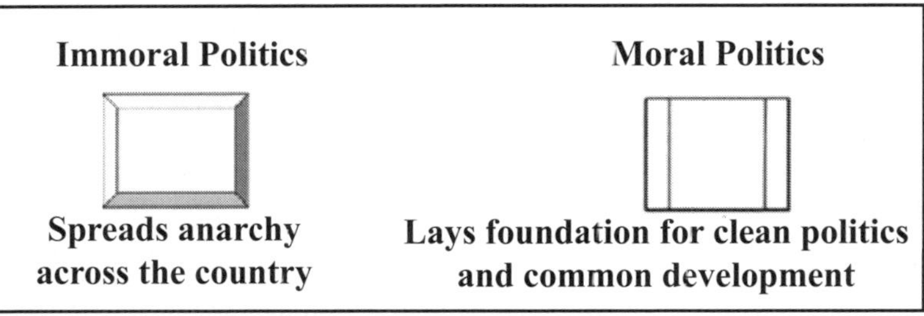

Lessons from Chanakya

Politics should always be centred on honesty. A righteous ruler always gets full support of the people of that country in all adversities. In politics, the primary goal of a ruler should always be welfare and prosperity for common people only. A ruler should be constantly striving for the welfare of people. The country should have an egalitarian society to ensure equal rights for all. Dishonesty and immoral behaviour of a person impacts his many generations. A politics, or for that matter any work based on immoral means never lasts long. Everybody should be honest and should follow righteousness. If a person is just honest and hard-working, he may attain all the pleasures of life. Not only that, his coming generations would also follow his footsteps.

❑

Joys and Sorrows of Life

Acharya's Pearls of Wisdom

• *Joys and sorrows and ups and downs keep coming in everybody's life. Instead of feeling helpless, a person should bravely face them.*

• *Six things that give worldly pleasure are - keeping good health, living without debts, not living in an alien country, company of noble persons, livelihood based on self-employment and living without fear.*

• *Six kinds of people who are always unhappy in this world are - envious people, people hating others, discontented people, angry persons, people always doubting others and people spending lives on other's fortunes.*

Joys and Sorrows

Meanings of joy and sorrow are different for different persons. A joy for somebody may become a reason for sorrow for another. A person who is potter by profession longs for bright sunshine to enable his pots to get dry whereas a farmer who has sown paddy desires for rains to have a good crop. In such a case, sunshine for one and rains for the other become the reason for despair. Today, we often find many people who get sad more by looking at the talent, success and happiness of others than by their own sorrow. Such people remain disturbed for their entire life. The real happiness is realised when a person envisions happiness for everybody and then endeavours to attain that happiness for all. Only animals look for food and pleasure for self, though even animals have feelings and, many a time, even they make arrangements for food for their ailing brethren. After all, we are humans. The very purpose of our human lives is to live a happy life together and serve our country.

A sportsman does not secure a gold medal just by making a solitary attempt; he needs to practise constantly. Non-success also means practice. Hence, people should remove 'non' from non-success and add practice to the same. It would thus be success + practice = triumph + happiness.

There is Nothing Called Non-success

For some, happiness depends primarily on success. Non-success upsets them and becomes a reason for their sorrow. This happens because people consider non-success as failures. They believe that they have failed in their endeavour whereas the reality is that there is nothing like failure in this life. There is also nothing like non-success in life and nobody succeeds in his first attempt. Some people, on failing in their first attempt, just stop moving ahead. Stopping to make an attempt, not failing in an attempt, is real non-success. If Thomas Alva Edison can fail 10,000 times before inventing an electric bulb, why not a common man? A sportsman does not secure a gold medal just by making a solitary attempt; he needs to practise constantly. Non-success also means practice. Hence, people should remove 'non' from non-success and add practice to the same. It would thus be success + practice = triumph + happiness.

The word 'non-success' is important only for those people who have mostly negative tendencies and somehow seek out negative points in every endeavour or situation. Discovery of the word 'non-success' also is a contribution of such people only with negative tendencies. People with positive attitude never treat non-success in a negative way. Chanakya also mentions that success in any endeavour is possible only with perfection. That person only who remains engaged in indefinite and impractical efforts fails to attain success and he only links non-success to failure. People who are highly determined and virtuous never stop trying until they attain complete success in their endeavours. On the other hand, there are also people who treat even a minor non-success as a major failure of their life and even go to the extent of ending their lives.

Suicide is definitely not a part of Indian culture. A person indulging in suicide actually commits a sin against his body, ruins the same. If a person stays undeterred in life and braves every problem with courage and self-confidence, he would not only attain all the happiness in life but also lead a respectable life. Life is a mixture of sweet and sour and combined together they give a great taste.

Suicide Because of Non-success

In today's world, suicide has become amajor issue. People instantly take recourse to suicide when they get hurt by their love affairs, examination results, jobs or relationships. Even Chanakya once encountered a similar situation. He was told that the state was witnessing a sudden spike in suicide incidents.

Chanakya asked the council of ministers about the reason for the same. The main reason that came out after deliberations was that people resorted to suicides as they were not happy and successful in their lives.

Chanakya said, "For this, we need to focus on economic development and welfare for common people." Additionally, he also advised to enact a law to prevent last rites for people resorting to suicides. People should be made aware that suicide is a grave crime. Joys and sorrows are the ways of live. Hence, people should learn to maintain harmony and balance with them. Suicide is definitely not a part of Indian culture. A person indulging in suicide actually commits a sin against his body, ruins the same. If a person stays undeterred in life and braves every problem with courage and self-confidence, he would not only attain all the happiness in life but also lead a respectable life. Life is a mixture of sweet and sour, and when combined together they give a great taste.

Thus, Chanakya did not consider even the last rites to be appropriate for people indulging in the heinous crime of suicide because of their non-success.

Non-success, many a time, also provides an indication of a change. When a person leads a monotonous life, his life becomes unexciting as the same lacks freshness. And lack of freshness results in lack of growth. The foundation of happiness is laid on non-success only. If the life of a person lacks this foundation, he would never perceive joys and sorrows in his life. Hence, it is necessary for a person to remain energetic and dynamic.

Joys and Sorrows Not The Only Goals of Life

Being happy is not the only purpose of life on this earth for a person. The life should have a meaningful purpose and contentment is the most important one for a person. Often, people waste years of their lives looking for happiness and then during their sunset years, they keep contemplating that they have still not attained that mirage they spent their precious years chasing. Money and wealth cannot provide happiness. Happiness is attained with contentment and happiness of mind. And mental peace and happiness is attained through noble deeds. If somebody is able to lessen the pain of a helpless and desolate soul lying on a road, he immediately gets a feeling of happiness.

A person sows the seeds of sorrow for himself when he, instead of giving attention to his own affairs and family, focuses on creating troubles for others. One may attain real happiness only when he joins others with a positive attitude and creates an environment of welfare for all.

Joys and Sorrows Self-created Sometimes

A person may attain joy and sorrow through himself also. One may find happiness even in helping helpless and incapable persons and also in providing education to illiterates. At the same time, if a person spends time in counting weak points of successful and accomplished individuals, he would be inviting troubles for himself. A person sows the seeds of sorrow for himself when he, instead of giving attention to his own affairs and family, focuses on creating troubles for others. One may attain real happiness only when he joins others with a positive attitude and creates an environment of welfare for all.

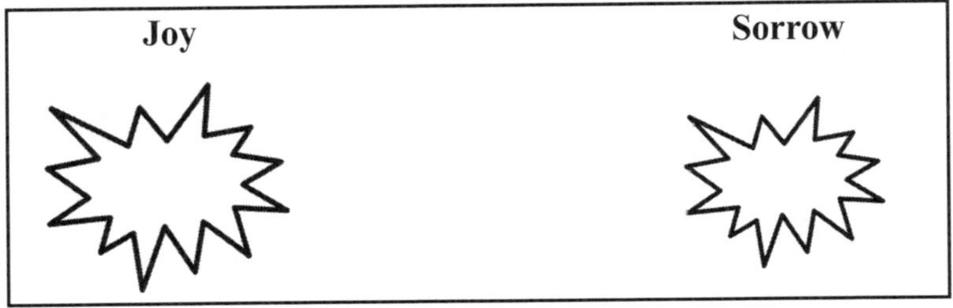

Lessons from Chanakya

There is nothing like non-success in life. Man should keep on moving ahead. Practice helps in keeping non-success at bay. Not only practice, one should ensure repetitive practice. Repetitive practice helps a person perfect even a difficult job. Concentration, diligence, righteousness and patience ensure persistent success in life. A person creates joys and sorrows for himself through his mind and deeds. If his mind is calm and peaceful, he finds joy and opportunity even in distress and problems. Hence, a person should keep focusing on his endeavours with right attitude.

❑

Clan and Caste

Acharya's Pearls of Wisdom

- *A scholar and virtuous person, even if low-born, may attain a respectable position in society.*
- *The grace of a family lies in its morality.*
- *Being high-born is not enough for a person to become great. For that, he also needs to be tolerant, patient, learned and philanthropic.*
- *Even a high-born person devoid of erudition and virtues has to face contemn.*

Chanakya had also made the same remark about man, "Good people are recognised by their values." One who gets enmeshed in kula, gotra and castes can never conquer the obstacle of his life. Rather than getting involved in the distinction of castes-varnas, he should lead his life with simplicity, dispassion and hard work to enjoy the same to the fullest.

Kula, Gotra and Caste

Humans existed on this earth even much before the written history itself came into existence. Humans then existed in the form of apes. It is widely believed that the modern humans came into existence some 2.5 million years age. The scientific name for human species is *Homo sapiens* i.e. wise man. *Homo* means humans and *sapiens* means intelligent. Signs of several species of humans like *Homo rudolfensis*, *Homo erectus* and *Homo neanderthalensis* are found on this earth. The most remarkable point common to all the above species was that these species had extraordinary brain capacity compared to other creatures. The brain provided humans the power and capacity to think and analyse. Gradual improvement in their level of intelligence helped humans to continue their evolutionary process. Discovery of fire and agricultural and other tools helped in providing a good degree of comfort to human life bit by bit. Earlier, humans were mainly engaged in looking for food, shelter and security. When the conditions gradually started to turn favourable, caste, religion, race, kula, gotra etc. also started receiving their attention. There was no religion on this earth in the beginning. It just happened that as humans marched ahead on their path of development, different groups of people brought into existence gods as per their preferences. Some people saw their gods in rocks, some others in scriptures while some of them saw gods in humans themselves.

Division of gotras was implemented when people of the same kula started to get divided into Kshatriya, Brahmin, Vaishya and Shudra. In such a case, it was only gotra that provided them identification. Varna caused creation of more castes and further division into upper and lower castes. Lower castes included the varnas that were engaged in menial jobs like cleaning, washing, shoe making, etc.

It's because of the divisions of kula, gotra and castes only that the incidents like honour killing continue to be national issues even today, whereas, Chanakya had centuries ago said, "A person gets disgraced not because he is low-born but because of his immoralities."

Man has himself created divisions of castes, religions, varnas and kulas. Every person gets born in the same way and his pace of development also is same as others. Everybody gets the same 24 hours in a day to work. He proves himself through his virtues and deeds only. Chanakya also had made the same remark about man, "Good people are recognised by their values." One who gets enmeshed in kula, gotra and castes can never conquer the obstacle of his life. Rather than getting involved in the distinction of castes-varnas, he should lead his life with simplicity, dispassion and hard work to enjoy the same to the fullest.

Varna-Related Issues Creeping Into Politics

Today, people don't hesitate in exploiting varna system to serve their own interests in politics. Incidents involving dalits and members of lower castes are promptly linked to politics. And in a very short time, these issues cross the limits of family and society and become national issues resulting in large-scale agitations. In India, such issues have not only created havoc in politics but also shaken the political system itself. Clean politics is generally based on the security and development of a country, but when the same gets trapped in castes, religions, kulas and gotras, the country deviates from its path of progress. Even today, caste-based occupations, caste-based reservations, caste-based politics and caste-based lifestyles are the reasons for aggravating social hostilities in our country. Political parties keep on inciting issues relating to caste-based reservations and the country remains busy in resolving such issues. Chanakya had considered Chandragupta suitable for the role of future emperor of Magadha based on his brilliance and will power. Chandragupta proved himself on all criteria set by Chanakya and Chanakya never gave any attention to his caste. All subsequent events are now parts of history. Chandragupta also honoured his Acharya and, under his guidance, proved himself as a great emperor whose regime is acclaimed all over the globe even today. Chanakya believed and knew that a person did not have to be high-born to become great; instead, he needs to be tolerant, patient, learned and philanthropic.

Chanakya maintains that if a person belonging to Shudra Varna develops his intelligence on the strength of his ability, talent and knowledge, even he becomes worthy of adoration like a Brahmin. At the same time, if a Brahmin indulges in lying and deceitful behaviour, he loses his right to be called a Brahmin. Nobody can be ostracised just because of his birth in a family with low social status.

Castes Are Based on Values

A person's caste depends on his values. Only values, deeds, knowledge, respect and attitude are the yardsticks of greatness. Chanakya maintains that if a person belonging to Shudra Varna develops his intelligence on the strength of his ability, talent and knowledge, even he becomes worthy of adoration like a Brahmin. At the same time, if a Brahmin indulges in lying and deceitful behaviour, he loses his right to be called a Brahmin. Nobody can be ostracised just because of his birth in a family with low social status. The same thing has also been mentioned in the conversation between Yidhisthira and Yaksha in *Mahabharata*, "A person does not become Brahmin just by birth. He does not become a Brahmin even just by acquiring knowledge of the Vedas. He rises to the position of a Brahmin only on account of his noble character. High moral character does not come from any specific caste; instead, it gets developed based on the values of the family. Jabali belonged to an unknown Varna but still his son Satyakam, because of his truthfulness and virtues, was considered to be worthy of Brahma-vidya. Growing expansion of education in our country is gradually bringing an end to caste-based activities. Today, a son of a shoemaker may rise to become an administrative officer while a Brahmin also may take up an employment. A person born in Kshatriya kula will definitely be very strong - this notion is no more tenable. People waste a major portion of their time in fighting these caste-related issues. If people start treating each other as equal and behave affectionately and in good faith, many of unwarranted problems of the country may vanish on their own.

Everybody tries to keep his place of residence and his surroundings clean to help him maintain healthy lifestyle in clean environment. In such a situation, dividing people based on man-made castes is irrelevant and unjustified. Many a time, seeds of inequality are sown in tender minds of low-born children from the very beginning. This results in development of inferiority complex in these children.

All Varnas Hidden in Every Person

Brahmin, Kshatriya, Vaishya and Shudra - these four varnas are present in every person. All these four varnas get assimilated in the person as he matures. When a person meditates with conviction and spirituality, he becomes a Brahmin. When the same person raises his voice against malpractices suffered by him or his family, he is called a Kshatriya. He takes the role of a Vaishya when he earns a livelihood to maintain his family. The same person becomes a Shudra when he uses a toilet. Everybody tries to keep his place of residence and his surroundings clean to help him maintain healthy lifestyle in clean environment. In such a situation, dividing people based on man-made castes is irrelevant and unjustified. Many a time, seeds of inequality are sown in tender minds of low-born children from the very beginning. This results in development of inferiority complex in these children. And hence, many a time, such children are not able to develop their qualities and skills in the absence of a proper environment. Children do not have any kula or religion. They should be allowed to bloom naturally. The same childhood blossoms to a fully developed flower and shoulders the responsibilities of a country.

Tyrannical Ruler Dhanananda, despite being a Kshatriya was not blessed with qualities of a king

Dhanananda was tyrannical and always indulged in luxuries. His only aim in life was self-gratification and hence he never paid attention to the problems of his subjects. Dhanananda had even insulted a scholar like Chanakya. Thus, despite being a Kshatriya, he was lacking in qualities of a king. We may also say that though he was high-born, he did not possess the values of a family with respectable high social status. History has record of many such rulers who shook the world and demeaned humanity with their immoral acts. At the same time, history is also replete with many other rulers who disseminated human values not only to their own kingdoms but also all across the world. The grandson of Chandragupta, Emperor Ashoka was unnerved by the results of wars and violence, by the blood-stained bodies of soldiers and by the screams of the wounded lying in the battlefield. He dedicated himself for the cause of non-violence. His ideas inspire not only India but also the entire world to follow the path of non-violence. His ideology of non-violence is firmly rooted in India as well as in the entire world even today.

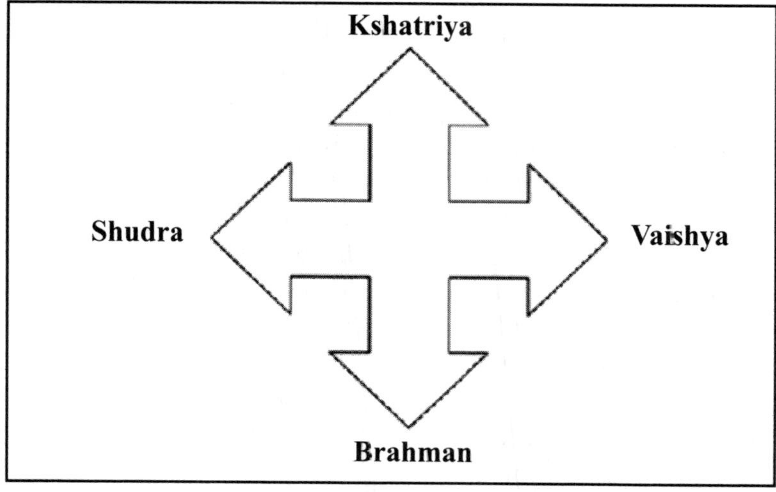

Every virtuous person is called high-born

Lessons from Chanakya

A person becomes great not because of his birth in a family with high status, rather he becomes great when he possesses virtuous qualities and adorns humanity irrespective of his lineage. A tolerant, patient, learned and philanthropic person is considered to be high-born. Man has created the system of varnas and religions for his own convenience. For a person who is humane and virtuous, his lineage does not have any importance. This was established by Chanakya centuries ago.

If people keep doing things with positive attitude using their intelligence, the disputes involving issues like religions, castes, kulas and gotras would never even get a chance to germinate.

❑

Chanakya and Gita

Acharya's Pearls of Wisdom

- *Man's fortune pays back according to his deeds.*
- *It's futile to wish for happiness after indulging in misdeeds.*
- *Man reaps what he sows.*
- *Compared to a long but purposeless life, a short life full of good deeds is much better.*

'Chanakya Niti', 'Arthashastra' and 'Gita'

Chanakya has, in his work '*Chanakya Niti*',shed light on almost all those topics that are covered in the Gita. '*Shrimad Bhagavad Gita*' and '*Chanakya Niti*' are very important pieces among Indian scriptures. It is widely believed that a person who goes through the *Gita* and the *Chanakya Niti* would never face defeat in his life. Chanakya himself, after completing his work *'Arthashastra'*, had clarified in *'Chanakya Niti'*, "Reading, understanding and assimilating the ideas in this treatise will enable even a common man to discern the difference between right and wrong and fair and unfair. My sole aim is to make people conscious of virtuousness, righteousness and their duties and responsibilities through this work." Chanakya was fully aware of the importance and relevance of *'Arthashastra'*. Hence, even for common people, he had said, "For common good, I am presenting all those hidden mysteries of politics that, if imbibed, would make a person omniscient. Success would undoubtedly chase the person who follows the moral principles enumerated in this treatise."

It will not be an exaggeration to say that *'Arthashastra'* is also considered one among the major scriptures of the world like *'Ramayana'*, *'Mahabharata'*, *'Guru Granth Sahib'*, *'Quran'* and *'Bible'*. Whereas *'Ramayana'*, *'Bible'* and *'Quran'* are mythological scriptures, the treatise *'Arthashastra'*, untying the knots of economic principles, is meant for the welfare of the entire humanity. Similarly, *'Gita'* explains the significance of conscientiousness for a person.

Resemblance Between *'Arthashastra'* and *'Gita'*

'Arthashastra': *'Arthashastra'* contains hidden mysteries of politics. Chanakya has used 'Kautilya' as his name in *'Arthashastra'*. The Kautilya's *Arthashastra* is divided into 15 books and 150 chapters. They contain detailed descriptions on duties of a king, selection of secret agents, selection of ministers, their periodic appraisals, armed forces, tax laws, land, supervision of fort and treasury, war, accord, identification of declared and disguised enemies, etc. Chanakya has also specified in the treatise how to be careful of the plotters. Not only that, even the ways to elude enemies and conspirators are mentioned in the same. Many of the secret mysteries have been uncovered in the book. Today, there is no clean and ideal politics in our country as well as in many other parts of the world because the principles of political science propounded in *'Arthashastra'* are not followed in those countries.

In *'Arthashastra'*, Chanakya has also elucidated in significant detail the methods of improving arts and crafts. He has not left any subject to be covered in *'Arthashastra'*. He has laid bare the conditions and characters of all the creatures in this living world, including the human world. How and what benefits man may avail out of forests, mines, etc. and how he may escape the onslaught of famines and natural calamities are all detailed in *'Arthashastra'*. The book has a mix of prose and poetry. Today, *'Arthashastra'* is available in different languages in simple but attractive forms to enable people with different native languages to reap benefit of the same.

*In **'Arthashastra'**, Chanakya has also elucidated in significant detail the methods of improving arts and crafts. He has not left any subject to be covered in **'Arthashastra'**. He has laid bare the conditions and characters of all the creatures in this living world, including the human world. How and what benefits man may avail out of forests, mines, etc. and how he may escape the onslaught of famines and natural calamities are all detailed in **'Arthashastra'**.*

Gita: The *Gita* presents the essence of a person's life. It is presumed to be authored by Veda Vyasa, though there is no conclusive evidence for the same. The text is based on the dialogue that took place between Arjuna and his charioteer Shri Krishna. The Gita has 18 chapters. Every chapter has answers to the questions related to a person's life. Jnana Yoga, Karma Yoga, Bhakti Yoga, Raja Yoga and monotheism are all explained very beautifully in the text. The first chapter of the *Gita* is *'Arjun Vishada Yoga'* or the 'Yoga of Arjun's Dejection'. 46 verses of the chapter present the state of mind of Arjuna. These verses try to exhibit the moral dilemmas faced by Arjuna. Seeing his relatives and friends on the enemy side, Arjuna gets distressed and refuses to fight. Krishna then explains to him that this world itself a Karmakshetra. In a Karmakshetra, one has to definitely fight for his rights and for protection of dharma on a right path.

The second chapter of the *Gita*, named as *'Sankhya Yoga'* has 72 verses. Shri Krishna, in this chapter, gives Arjuna lessons on Karma Yoga, Jnana Yoga, Sankhya Yoga, Buddhi Yoga and self-knowledge. This chapter has the essence of the Gita. The third chapter is *Karma Yoga*. Here, Shri Krishna explains to Arjuna the importance of karma (action) and tells him that every person should keep on doing their duty without craving for results. The action bears appropriate fruits at appropriate time automatically. In the fourth chapter, Shri Krishna spells out the importance of guru. In the fifth chapter, Shri Krishna tells Arjuna that karma yoga is better for life. In the sixth chapter, Shri Krishna elucidates details of Ashtang Yoga and explains how man should keep the dilemmas of mind at bay. Seventh chapter titled as *'Jnana-Vijnana'* contains Shri Krishna's teachings on reality and delusion. In the eighth chapter *'Aksara-Brahma Yoga'*, he throws light on the hell and the heaven.

Similarly, Shri Krishna talks about other aspects of life in the rest of ten chapters. At some point, he displays his universal form (Visvasvarupa) while some other time he speaks about the best, average and other forms of tyagaa, renunciation and abandonment.

Similarities Between Chanakya and Shri Krishna

Shri Krishna: Shri Krishna had divine powers. He was proficient in sixteen kalas. He had deep understanding of all the aspects of life. He also had realisation of the results of immorality and kindness. He was dark coloured. Shri Krishna would initially try to resolve an issue in the normal course. If unsuccessful, he would use tact to resolve the same. If the issue still remained unresolved, he treated war as the ultimate course to resolve the same.

Shri Krishna had divine powers. He was proficient in sixteen kalas. He had deep understanding of all the aspects of life. He also had realisation of the results of immorality and kindness. He was dark coloured. Shri Krishna would initially try to resolve an issue in the normal course.

Chanakya: Chanakya was a great scholar. Despite being a normal human, he was blessed with supernatural powers on account of his education. He was extremely clever just like Shri Krishna. Chanakya also followed the principle of Saam, Daam, Dand and Bhed. If enemies accepted their fault easily, Chanakya would not use other methods, but if they did not submit despite all efforts, Dand or war was the only recourse. Both Shri Krishna and Chanakya had the same goal viz. protection of common people, establishment of a welfare state and installation of an ideal ruler. Both considered life to be karma-oriented and karma-determined. Both believed that fortune is built on the foundations of karma. As you sow, so shall you reap. This is as realistic and effective today as it was during the times of Krishna and Chanakya.

Significance of *'Gita'* and *'Arthashastra'* in our daily life

The *Gita* and the *Arthashastra* appear to be quite complex to people in general. Today, many simple forms of these books are also available in market. The *Gita* and the *Arthashastra* have been presented in summarised forms in simple language to enable common people to leverage the teachings in their daytoday lives.

Prominent Points of 'Gita' and 'Chanakya Niti'

Chanakya has presented extraordinarily shrewd thoughts in a compendious form in *'Chanakya Niti'*. The same points have been discussed in the Gita also.

Gita	Chanakya Niti
Emphasis on karma by a peson	Arthashastra provides tips to do karma cleverly.
Keep anger under control. Anger leads a person to destruction. Anger and fear are our enemies.	Anger is a strong poison. This completely ruins a person.
This body is made of fire, water, air, earth and sky and will ultimately dissolve into them. a sould never dies. Hence enjoy this life with self-realisation.	The soul inside our body is a river. This river originates from the body of God. Patience forms its bonlers, compassion its stream and virtúes its piligrimage.
One should not live in the past or worry about the future as, what is destinaed will sourely happen. Hence, enjoy the present.	A prudent person lives in the present and makes his life meaningful.

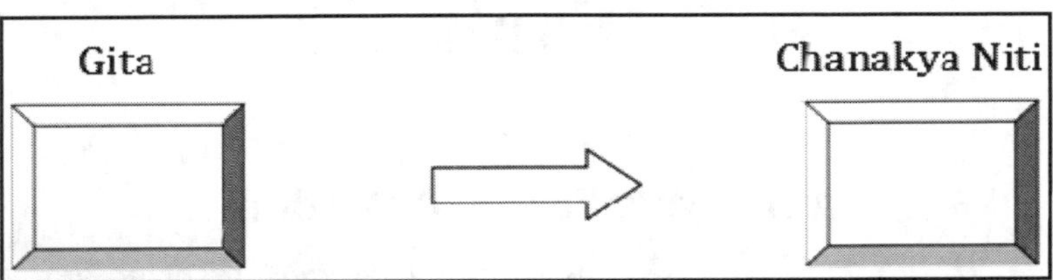

Equality and Importance

Lessons from Chanakya

This world is a Karmakshetra. Here, what a person reaps in his life depends on his deeds, lifestyle, education and behaviour. If a person indulges in betraying humanity with his negative and violent notions, he deserves punishment. Fortune depends on karma. Hence, everybody should perform his karma with purity, fairness and honesty.

❑

Fault

Acharya's Pearls of Wisdom

- *If a babul shrub remains leafless even during spring, it's not the fault of spring.*
- *It's useless to fault sun for an owl's inability to see in the daytime.*
- *Clouds can't be blamed if raindrops do not fall into the mouth of a skylark.*

Fault And the Defaulter

Fault is a word that encapsulates multiple meanings. It may mean shortcoming, crime, mistake, malfunction, blemish, guilt, etc. This may be used in different ways.

First usage - Assume two friends have agreed to meet at a location. But, the train taken by one friend gets delayed. The other friend gets displeased over the delay. In such a situation, the first friend would say, "The train did not arrive at the right time. Where is my fault?"

Second usage - An officer assigns an important task to a person. That person, however, forgets to complete the task. The officer says, "This task was assigned to you. You only are at fault for not completing the same."

Third usage - Two persons are bad-mouthing some third person, "Hey, I do not even talk to him. He has got many faults."

Fourth usage - "Please do not fault me for lying."

Here, the word fault refers to an offence in the first sentence, a mistake in the second, a shortcoming in the third and a blemish in the fourth sentence.

Nobody wants to be at fault but a strong desire to fault others is found in every person having negative attitude. People who have positive predisposition and are brimming with self-confidence have the power to refuse to be at fault. They use all of their strength to make even an impossible task possible.

Faulty Muhurta, Fate and Seasons

It is said that both cockroach and human being are the creatures that know how to live in any condition. A human being is very selfish by nature. He tries to mould every situation in his favour, though a situation can't be moulded just by a desire. That requires tough struggle, hard work and strong will power on the part of that person. People with weak will power blame circumstances for their failures at the drop of a hat.

Muhurta, fate and season - these three elements are used quite frequently by a common man. When he wants to avoid hard work or when he does not want to take responsibility for his failures, he simply puts blame on muhurta, fate and season. Man is very clever. He knows well that muhurta, fate and season are such elements that would never be able to open their mouth; their existence has been created and lodged in his imagination. There is no existence of muhurta, fate and season for a person who is always eager to do something great with resolve and strong will power in his mind. Such a person carries his muhurta, fate and season with him. Wherever he sets his foot with honesty and self-confidence, muhurta, fate and season also come into existence at that place.

There is no existence of muhurta, fate and season for a person who is always eager to do something great with resolve and strong will power in his mind. Such a person carries his muhurta, fate and season with him. Wherever he sets his foot with honesty and self-confidence, muhurta, fate and season also come into existence at that place.

Chanakya had realised this centuries ago that if a person failed to accomplish something, it never meant that he should blame conditions or other individuals for the same and prove himself innocent.

It is the mind of a person that determines a victory or defeat. Napoleon Hill has also mentioned, "A person's mind may turn a heaven into hell and a hell into heaven."

Here are some such incidents only that happened during 2019 where individuals refused to accept defeat with the wit of their minds.

Human Brain - An Extremely Powerful Tool

A person may change history with his intelligence, wisdom, courage and deeds. Chanakya says that the person who tries to live a life of fate actually spoils his precious life futilely. It is the mind of a person that determines a victory or defeat. Napoleon Hill has also mentioned, "A person's mind may turn a heaven into hell and a hell into heaven."

Here are some such incidents only that happened during 2019 where individuals refused to accept defeat with the wit of their minds.

Example 1: Vinayak Sreedhar of India was suffering from 'muscular dystrophy' right from the age of 2 years. This disorder is characterised by progressive muscle degeneration and weakness. It drastically shortens life of the afflicted person. Vinayak was aware that he was not going to survive for long but still he refused to bow down to fate and circumstances. He continued to study hard. People used to get amazed to see his talent. He appeared for examination for three subjects for 10th standard - English, Sanskrit and History. He left for heavenly abode before he could take the rest of the papers. Vinayak secured very good marks in all three subjects.

Example 2: Shubham lost both his hands and one leg in an accident. It can be only imagined how difficult it would have been to lead a normal life with only one leg. However, with his will power, Shubham used that single leg itself as his hand as well as his leg. He cleared the examination for 10th standard using that single leg only. Today, he is able to operate his laptop and mobile also with that leg only.

Example 3: The life of Jessica Cocks of the United States of America is not only inspirational for everybody but that also strongly supports the belief that if a person is mentally strong, he can make his disability itself his weapon and forget the words like fault or defaulter. Jessica Cocks was born without hands. Initially, her parents got artificial hands fixed just to avoid her having any inferiority complex. However, Jessica felt quite uncomfortable with those artificial hands. Hence, she gradually learnt to use her legs for all her personal activities. She would take care of all her jobs right from reading books to having meals, combing hairs etc. with the help of her legs. She even started to participate in dance competitions in her school. She secured championship in Karate using her legs only. She learnt horse riding and scuba diving with her those very legs. Along with all these things, she also continued with her studies and secured graduation degree in Psychology. With passage of time, her passion for learning something new kept on growing further. She started to drive her car and do typewriting with her legs only. At the age of 25 years, she thought of flying aeroplanes and decided to become a pilot. She went for training for the same. The plane used for her training required only two hands and not legs for control. However, as Jessica did not have hands, she had to make do with her legs only. She took control of the plane with her legs only. She started training under the guidance of three trainers. She took some three years to learn flying. During that period, she had to often go for training flights extending to many hours. Ultimately, she achieved what others are unable to achieve even with both their hands intact. She secured the license to fly lightweight aeroplanes. Thus, she became an extraordinary woman pilot flying aeroplanes with her legs only. Jessica Cocks was proactive. She would say, "I never allowed the circumstances and my disabilities to make me believe that I could not accomplish anything as I did not have hands. I always had the conviction that I could do anything. I am not inferior to anybody in this world."

Jessica Cocks was proactive. She would say, "I never allowed the circumstances and my disabilities to make me believe that I could not accomplish anything as I did not have hands. I always had the conviction that I could do anything. I am not inferior to anybody in this world." If a person has passion, the Nature teaches him everything.

If a person has passion, nature teaches him everything. Today, Jessica Cocks, with her unparalleled achievements, is leading a successful and happy married life. Her friend Patrick Chamberlane decided in 2012 to marry her. However, as Jessica did not have hands, how could he put the ring on her finger? Noticing the sign of predicament on his face, Jessica moved her leg forward and

Patrick put the wedding ring on a finger of her leg and made her his life partner.

Henry David Thoreau says, "In my knowledge, there is nothing more encouraging than the fact that man has undisputed ability to lift the quality of his life with a conscious effort."

Example 4: 52-year-old blind sailor from Japan, Mitsuhiro Iwamoto successfully completed a near two-month, nonstop voyage of 14000 km to cross Pacific Ocean on his 12m long sailboat. He is the first person in the world to accomplish this.

All the above individuals, had they so wished, could have easily put blame on fate and somehow kept on dragging their lives. However, they just got rid of the notion that they had any fault. These people always had the belief in their mind that they could do anything.

Throw Away Negative Words Like 'Fault' and 'Defaulter'

Negative words cripple even the nervous system of our brain. Hence, make your vocabulary positive and throw away from your life all such negative words that create hurdles for your growth. Everything in this world is achievable. One has to just have a positive passion to achieve the same.

Negative words cripple even the nervous system of our brain. Hence, make your vocabulary positive and throw away from your life all such negative words that create hurdles for your growth. Everything in this world is achievable. One has to just have a positive passion to achieve the same.

Chanakya maintains that a talented, educated, intelligent and knowledgeable person is always respected. That's why, the entire earth as also the entire universe is always ready with open arms to help such people.

Break Out of Your Comfort Zone

Chanakya feels that a prudent and intelligent person should not get perturbed by problems and difficulties. He should brave them with fearlessness, self-confidence and patience. People with weak disposition get worried when faced with problems. They feel afraid to take bold steps alone. The term 'people with weak disposition' refers to people who are easy-going, lazy, wicked, immoral and irresponsible. These people like to create hurdles for energetic and hard-working people and try to inflict harm on them. Such people with weak disposition just keep on dreaming of great things for themselves but in reality, they never try to make any good and bold attempt. Such people get trapped in a circle on this earth. People themselves, not the nature, have made this circle. As the number of people grows in this circle, the fights among them also grow. On the contrary, a virtuous, prudent, knowledgeable and focussed person brimming with self-confidence keeps on making efforts to develop himself and the country without paying any attention to others. The earth undoubtedly embraces such people wholeheartedly. That is the reason that such determined people are able to uproot any problem or obstacle out of their ways. This happens because they are different from the people with weak disposition imprisoned in the circle. They have to neither pull down nor bad-mouth anybody. They just know how to make their lives meaningful and how to win themselves in every situation. Chanakya maintains that a talented, educated, intelligent and knowledgeable person is always respected. That's why, the entire earth as also the entire universe is always ready with open arms to help such people.

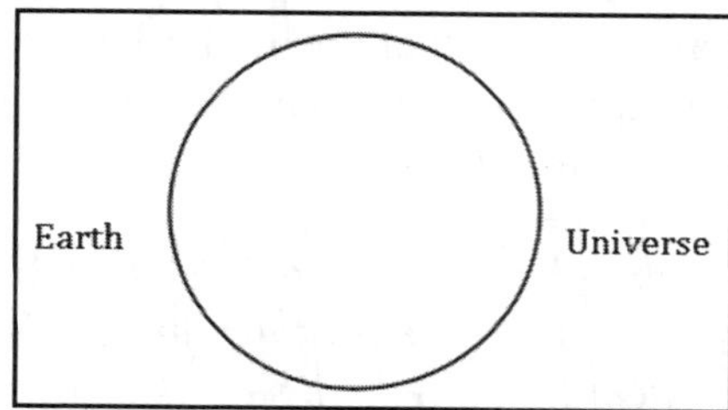

People with weak disposition imprisoned in circle

Lessons from Chanakya

There is open sky for everybody on this earth. Every person may not only lead his life as per his aspirations but may also, on the strength of his deeds, offer something to this world for common good. The person who puts blame for his failures on fate, muhurta, season or other people is indolent, lazy and a burden on this earth. Many different words for 'fault' are applicable only to such people with indolent and lethargic tendencies. And the people, who are confident to be able to bring down the sky, shake the abyss and change the direction of wind, remove the word 'fault' from their lives. With the help of their diligence and struggle, they make themselves so capable that the word like 'fault' can't at all be foisted on them. Life is very beautiful. This should be lived to the fullest.

❑

A Book Never Ends

A book is everything for a man - a friend, a guide as well as a companion. We have written so many texts and words in our lives. Out of all of them, the most favourite word for people is 'love'. People like everything talked about love viz. love is blind or love transforms a person completely etc. etc.

While remembering Romeo-Juliet, Shirin-Farhad and Laila-Majnu, have you ever wondered why only a male and a female are mentioned in love stories or why such love stories only are found to be fascinating and interesting by people. Love is just love and anybody may fall in love anytime and anywhere.

Have you ever heard of any person who got attracted to something other than his opposite sex? Just take an example of a book. Wait! Are you by any chance wondering what kind of topic I have taken up for discussion at the end of this book? If it is really so, it's not surprising. Anybody would feel like that only. What I am going to tell you may be a real surprise for you.

The attraction between opposite sexes is normal and straight forward. For once, get into the attraction of a book and feel its magic. Try to feel those black letters that, when read, brighten your life. Write white letters on the slate of your life. Reading and writing always enhance the intelligence and prudence of a person and make his thoughts mature. When that person wholeheartedly imbibes matured thoughts, he gets highly spirited. Such a person single-handedly dazzles the universe with his talent and becomes immortal for centuries.

We have heard the word 'magic' quite often during our childhood. What is there in magic? Magic mostly entails mesmerising the audience with attempts involving tricks to make supernatural feats look real and natural. Magic is used to bring fantasies down to the horizon of realism.

Books also have similar magic but, to understand and realise that magic, a person must love the books just the way a man loves his beloved. People in love, despite being away from their partners, always have the feeling of their close proximity. Books also have the same intoxication, love and magic. Books talk to you, love you. When you read them with pure heart and get deep into them, they constantly stand by you to save you from drowning in the sea of problems. Books always protect their readers, just as a man and his beloved take care of each other.

It was only after realising the importance of books that Chanakya put down all his experience in politics and economy in black and white in the form of his great work *'Arthashastra'* to enable people to use this as a medium to improve their lives.

When a book comes in hand, it definitely gets a start but it never ends. This happens because when a person goes through magical words in the book and tries to imbibe the ideas, he encounters many fresh experiences and realities. These experiences and realities prompt his pen to start again from the point where the book had concluded, to make a new beginning and provide its readers something good and interesting to read.

The attraction between opposite sexes is normal and straight forward. For once, get into the attraction of a book and feel its magic. Try to feel those black letters that, when read, brighten your life. Write white letters on the slate of your life. Reading and writing always enhance the intelligence and prudence of a person and make his thoughts mature. When that person wholeheartedly imbibes matured thoughts, he gets highly spirited. Such a person single-handedly dazzles the universe with his talent and becomes immortal for centuries. Chanakya had also done the same thing only. Hence, he became immortal not only in India and not only abroad but in the entire universe. What's the delay then? Go through this book and relate all the great ideas of Chanakya to your life. You would soon find that your life has turned extremely beautiful and magical.

❑❑❑